Sir Richard Hill

Deep Things of God - Or Milk and Strong Meat

Containing Spiritual and Experimental Remarks and Meditations,

Sir Richard Hill

Deep Things of God - Or Milk and Strong Meat
Containing Spiritual and Experimental Remarks and Meditations,

ISBN/EAN: 9783337115241

Printed in Europe, USA, Canada, Australia, Japan

Cover: Foto ©Lupo / pixelio.de

More available books at **www.hansebooks.com**

DEEP THINGS OF GOD;

OR,

MILK AND STRONG MEAT:

CONTAINING

SPIRITUAL AND EXPERIMENTAL REMARKS AND MEDITATIONS,

SUITED

TO THE CASES OF BABES, YOUNG MEN, AND FATHERS IN CHRIST:

PARTICULARLY,

TO SUCH AS ARE UNDER TRIALS AND TEMPTATIONS, AND WHO FEEL THE PLAGUE OF THEIR OWN HEARTS.

I will never leave thee, nor forsake thee. DEUT. xxxi. 6, 8.
HEB. xiii. 5.
When thou passest through the waters, I will be with thee; and through the rivers, they shall not overflow thee: when thou walkest through the fire, thou shalt not be burnt; neither shall the flame kindle upon thee.
ISA. xliii. 2.

LONDON:
Printed for J. MATHEWS, Bookseller, No. 18, Strand.
M.DCC.LXXXVIII.

PREFACE.

THE following remarks and meditations were most of them written down, when I felt the power and sweetness of them upon my own soul.

As they were put to paper without order or connection, so neither elegance or connection must be expected in the reading of them.

I am sensible that they contain *strong and savory meat*, and such as many, who are as yet but babes in Christ, cannot digest; much less will they be relished by the children of this world; and least of all will they go down with the modern Pharisee, the strutting daw in Christian plumes, who, *having the form of godliness, but denying the power,* can but ill brook any exhortations to heavenly-mindedness, or close walking with God. He tells you " he " would have every body be good, and " mind their duty; and all pretensions " beyond this, he is sure, are the effect of " hypocrisy and precisenes." Then, as to spiritual desertions and consolations, these things, he is certain, are the mere whims of melancholy and enthusiasm: with regard to regeneration, we were all born again in baptism; and, for his part, he has no notion of *inward feelings.* But worst of all can he bear the sound of Salvation by Grace. His very heart rises at the declaration, when he hears, that the most profligate and abandoned

sinners

sinners of mankind have as free a welcome to all gospel blessings, without waiting for any amendment, as the strictest moralist upon earth. "Let who will be-
"lieve such extravagant opinions, he makes
"no doubt, but piety, virtue, and good
"works (offered up through the merits
"of Christ) will recommend us to the favor of the *Deity*; and he is persuaded,
"that every man of sense, and who is possessed with goodness of heart and liberality of sentiment, must be of the same
"mind with himself. Indeed he cannot
"think otherwise, without professing himself an enemy to morality, and without
"harboring the most injurious notions of
"the *Supreme Being.*" Thus he believes *something*, he hardly knows what, *about* the scriptures; however he readily persuades himself, that he is a Christian, and in the way to heaven, till, in the solemn moment
of

of departure, he lifts up his eyes and cries, *behold it was a dream!*

But though all the ungodly upon earth should scoff; though the multitude of Formalists should rage and swell; yet I am persuaded, that poor, convinced, humbled sinners, and especially tempted souls fighting with besetting sins, and groaning for deliverance, will feed on the honey which these observations will, I trust, be found to contain, and will find them *precious to their taste; a feast of fat things, of wine on the lees well refined.* My wish, however, is, that they may be taken all together, collectively, and that no judgment may be formed of any of them separately. In this view, I doubt not, but every experienced believer will set his seal to the truth of every one of them.

That

That no poor foul, who has received the grace of God in truth, may be tempted to defpair on account of the prevalence of corruption, great care is taken to point out the difference between the falls of a believer and an unbeliever, as well by defcribing the actings of mind both of the one and of the other, under fuch circumftances, as the ftate of their perfons Godward. The latter (the unbeliever) condemned by the holy law, and deftitute of a principle of grace, finking by his falls, like *lead in the mighty waters* : The former, (the believer) fcreened from the curfe of the law, by that divine righteoufnefs, which cannot be fullied by fin, and which is proof againft all the attacks of Satan's malice, refembling wood, which though repeatedly dafhed by violence into the ocean, and immerfed for a time under the waves, as often rifes up again by the power of its own proper specific tendency to mount upwards.

Various as the trials and temptations of God's children are, according to their circumstances, constitutions and situations in life, it is hoped that every one will find something in the following pages suited to his own particular state; for though the Lord in his wisdom and love always fits each trial, however sore and grievous, to each believer, and each believer to each trial which is allotted to him, yet there is but one way of deliverance under all, which is by *looking to Jesus*, and acting faith on the word of promise.

I am aware, that the same sentiments and ideas will be found in many of the Numbers, particularly in those which treat of justification, faith, and repentance; but as

they

they are reprefented in different points of view, and juft as they occurred to my own mind, I hope that whatever there is of repetition, inftead of being tirefome, will tend to the greater confirmation of truth, and the more firm eftablifhment of the believer's foul in folid peace, comfort and holinefs.

It is now more than thirty years that the Lord has been training me up in the fchool of experience, and it is almoft thofe many years that feveral of the following obfervations were put down in different diaries, merely for my own ufe, without the leaft defign of making them public; though the various ftates, temptations, and viciffitudes I have gone through (Jehovah's love ftill remaining unchangeable) has greatly fwelled the volume. A few judicious Chriftians, to whom I communicated a

part

part of the manuscript, having expressed much satisfaction in the perusal of it, I came to the resolution of printing it, and made some considerable addition to it; with no other view and design that what proceeded from the hope, that the whole might be made profitable to that church, which God the Redeemer hath purchased with his own blood.

ERRATA.

Page 17, line 19, before *with* add *and*.
Page 17, line 26, for *acting* read *actings*.
Page 47, line 20, for *will ever* read *shall ever*.
Page 77, line 4, for *raises* read *rises*.
Page 114, line 3, for SPIRITUAL read GRADUAL.
Page 117, line 12, for *become* read *became*.
Page 127, for *there whilst* read *whilst there*.

REMARKS,

Remarks, Meditations, &c.

No. I.

HOW long might one live with some persons who are looked upon as very good Christians, and not know whether they had any souls or not!

No. II.

THE enmity there is in the fallen heart of man to God, will ever shew itself against Christ's faithful people. Self-love and self-deceit are the parents of this hatred which the world shews towards real Christians.

No. III.

No. III.

AS the praife of true religion is not of men but of God, fo there certainly is *a thing* called Religion which will pleafe the world, whofe praife is not of God but of men: but the down-right libertine and the real Chriftian will both be difapproved of, though the latter more than the former.

No. IV.

IF a man fhew not what is generally thought too great a conformity to the image of Chrift, nor too little conformity to the ways of the world, that man will be idolized; but then it muft be obferved, that this love towards him does not arife from what the people of the world fee in him agreeable to the tempers of Jefus Chrift, but from what they perceive in him correfpondent with their own fentiments and conduct, whilft the holy, wary walk of the true believer, is as a thorn in the fide of every counterfeit profeffor.

No. V.

No. V.

"THAT Religion (if so it must be called) which a man keeps to himself, or which is confined to acts of kindness towards the body, will never cause the least offence; but in proportion as any person is active in furthering the salvation of others, he is sure of making himself obnoxious to the eyes of the world.

No. VI.

THE image of God, stamped upon the new-born soul, is what the most double refined formalist cannot bear, for as much as a vital Christian is a living reproof to all such skeletons of piety. Hence it is that they frequently gainsay, and oppose what in their own hearts they dreadfully mistrust to be right: and though they hate the holiness of God's children, yet have they a kind of devilish and malicious pleasure whenever they can pick out any failings or infirmities to reproach them with.

No. VII.

IF you will be the world's favorite, you muſt neither be too like God, nor too like the devil.

No. VIII.

SOME people are mightily offended at the word *ſaint* : a ſad proof that they themſelves have no title to the character; but ſure it is, that every perſon living is either a ſinner or a ſaint. The former all men are by nature, the latter a choſen few are by grace; yet a believer is ſtill a ſinner, though not under condemnation for ſin.

The word ſaint, from *ſanctus*, means nothing but an holy perſon; and an holy perſon, in the ſcripture account, is a believer and no other. So that whoever diſclaims the denomination of a Saint, thereby acknowledges himſelf to be under the curſe of God, and to have no right or title to any of the goſpel bleſſings.

The word of God knows no ſuch diſtinctions as virtuous men and vicious men, moral and immoral, &c. &c. but ranks the whole world into two claſſes, viz. believers and unbelievers; children of light, and children of darkneſs; regenerate and carnal, ſinners and ſaints.

The one accepted in Chriſt Jeſus: the other having the wrath of God abiding on them.

No. IX.

HEART-ſearching preaching, where it does not convince, is ſure to offend. Nothing is ſo cutting to an unrenewed heart, eſpecially where there is a decent outſide, as to have it's rottenneſs expoſed, it's refuge of lies ſwept away, and the pillow of forms, whereon it was ſleeping, removed from under the head. Whoſoever attempts this muſt expect to ſee the old man riſe and fume, ſince to approve the real chriſtian, and the real truth, would cauſe the Phariſee to condemn himſelf.

No. X.

THE moſt dangerous infidels are not the moſt open infidels. There is a ſet of men, who perſuade themſelves that they believe chriſtianity, whilſt in truth they are reaſoning chriſtianity quite out of doors.

No. XI.

WHAT pains do some parents take to teach their children the catechism, to make them repeat prayers night and morning, and to bring them to church, perhaps to sacrament, who yet would be very uneasy and much displeased to see those children become real children of God living by faith above the world.

No. XII.

THERE may be a great deal of morality where there is no true religion; but there can be no true religion where there is no morality.

No. XIII.

WHAT avails it to attend constantly upon church and sacrament, to be liberal in our alms-deeds, and diligent in reading the scriptures, if we are not *created anew in Christ Jesus?* St. Paul makes no difference between the vilest profligate and

and the faireſt moraliſt, but ranks all without exception under the liſt of *reprobates* who have not *Jeſus Chriſt in them.* 2 Cor. xiii. 5. So alſo the ſame apoſtle aſſures us that *if any man* (be he ever ſo ſtrict, devout and decent) *have not the ſpirit of Chriſt, he is none of his.* Rom. viii. 9. The word of God makes it abſolutely neceſſary that *Chriſt be formed in us.* Gal. iv. 9. and without this ſpiritual birth, eternal truth repeatedly aſſures us that *we cannot enter into the kingdom of heaven.* John iii. 3, 4, 5, 6.

No. XIV.

THERE is a great deal of difference between praying and ſaying of prayers. There are many who never omit falling on their knees night and morning, and repeating a certain number of words, who never prayed in all their lives. They often carry petitions to God that have no reference to their own caſe, and look upon their prayers rather as gifts that they bring to him, than as means in the uſe of which they expect to receive any thing from him.

The heart may pray where there are no audible words, as in the caſe of *Hannah.* 1 Sam. i. 13. and ſuch prayer ſhall find acceſs to the throne

throne of grace; and, *vice versâ*, there may be many words without any thing of the spirit of prayer accompanying them.

XV.

WHEN a poor unawakened soul, who has long lingered under some bodily disease dies, it is often said " it is happy for such a one that he is released."

No. XVI.

AS some things become petrified by the frequent dropping of water upon them, so some persons who have sat long under the word faithfully preached, without being converted, become more and more hardened.

No. XVII.

NOMINAL, lukewarm christians are perhaps worse enemies to religion than professed infidels, and are generally the most bitter persecutors that the people of God meet with.

No. XVIII.

No. XVIII.

SOME people, especially those *who have a name to live, and are dead*, are so exceedingly averse to be brought to the knowledge of themselves, and to lose the good opinion they have formed of their own excellencies, that they cannot bear to see the corruption and rottenness of their own hearts, and are highly offended at the faithfulness of any minister who would strip off their varnish, and shew them to themselves in their true colors.

No. XIX.

SCARCELY two persons run the same road to destruction; but there is but one way to happiness—*I am the way*, saith Christ.

No. XX.

WHEN it is said "such or such persons have never seen any thing of the world," it generally

means

means that they have never been led about to play-houses, balls, routs, &c. and have no acquaintance with what is commonly called *the best company*, in other words (too often) the most worthless and the most profligate part of the creation.

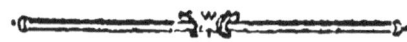

No. XXI.

HOW many people are there whose hearts are as much glued to the world as possible, who neverthelefs fancy that they are entirely difentangled from it?

No. XXII.

IN most cases, we ought to weigh our intentions, before we put them into execution, to fee whether we run any risk in offending God in what we are about to do; but where our fleshly lusts are concerned, it is quite otherwise: the less we argue and deliberate, the better. Whilst we are debating, our passions are kindling, so that reasoning with ourselves here, is like flinging oil upon fire in order to extinguish it.—But flight and prayer are special helps.

No. XXIII.

THERE are few sinners but what hope to repent before they die, and neverthelefs continue to swallow the damnable intoxicating draughts of sin. The extravagant folly of such persons may be compared to that of a man who stabs himself in order to heal the wound again.

No. XXIV.

THERE are those who plunge themselves deeper and deeper into sin, in order to stifle the thoughts of those sins which they have already committed: this is just as if a man should drink one dose of poison in order to expel another.

No. XXV.

THERE are perhaps more souls lost through a false confidence of salvation, than by any other deceit the Devil makes use of: I mean not

amongst

amongst notorious sinners, but among the more decent formalists, who, because they have never fallen into any foul, gross sins, or because their lives are somewhat reformed, and they practise some outward duties, make no doubt of the safety of their state: whereas they have no union with Christ by faith; the great renovating change has never been wrought in them; their natures are still unrenewed, their hearts unsanctified; they never saw and bewailed their own vileness; they never felt their real need of a Saviour, in a way of renunciation of their own righteousness; nor do they pant and labour after higher degrees of grace and holiness, like a true child of God, who can never rest contented with his present attainments; but they keep plodding on in the same beaten track, vainly thinking to divide their hearts between God and the world; and contenting themselves with a formal, lifeless, luke-warm religion, which only tends to their greater delusion; and thus they go on dreaming of heaven till they awake in hell.

XXVI.

BECAUSE our blessed Lord, his apostles and prophers have said such and such things, many think they believe them, when in truth they do nothing lefs. The reafon why they fo deceive themfelves, is, that what they read in the fcripture, they readily make bend to their own fancies; but were they to hear the very fame words from any minifter of the gofpel in a fermon, or to read them in any evangelical author, they would immediately exclaim againft them, as Methodifm, Enthufiafm, Calvinifm, Antinomianifm, and what not.

To make us believe God's word upon its own record, and upon its own authority, requires a power more than human.

No. XXVII.

EXHORTATIONS to forfake fin, and to obey God, upon Arminian Principles, never can be attended with any good fuccefs, feeing they neither fhew man the depth of his difeafe, nor the freenefs, fullnefs, and all-fufficiency of the Gofpel falvation: fo that he neither knows his own utter helplefinefs, nor where all his ftrength lies.

No. XXVIII.

No. XXVIII.

WHAT pains do many lukewarm profeſſors take to keep themſelves faſt aſleep in carnal ſecurity! If they ſee their wretched caſe laid open by any Chriſtian writer, or faithful Miniſter, either they are ready to carp or quarrel with ſuch, or to conclude, that they themſelves know better, that the man is miſtaken, and that there is no need of ſo much ſtrictneſs and preciſeneſs, nor of that wonderful change of heart which only a few enthuſiaſts here and there make ſo abſolutely neceſſary to ſalvation; but on the contrary, when they hear any formal, daubing, unawakened miniſter preach, or read any dry lifeleſs (wrongly called *religious*) book, how eager are they to catch at whatever may ſooth them in their deluſion! and are as much pleaſed with thoſe who help to lull them in their fatal dream, as a child is pleaſed to be lulled aſleep by the fables and tales of its nurſe.

No. XXIX.

No. XXIX.

THOUGH the Lord will never remember the sins of a believer, to his condemnation; yet the believer himself will always remember them to his humiliation.

No. XXX.

IT is not uncommon to hear Professors say, that "they have done with looking to frames and feelings; and what they depend on is the unchangeable promise of God."

This *may* be the language of sound tried faith in the furnace; but I believe it is oftener the language of a spiritual decline, or of a loose, careless walk. Whoever wishes to live near to God, and to have communion and fellowship with him, will put the highest value upon the sensible comforts of his Spirit.

We may set up distinctions about walking by faith and walking by sight, and there may be times and cases in which this distinction is to be attended to: but I can see no reason why the man who is strong in faith, should not also be *filled with joy and peace in believing*.

That is an unscriptural notion which would separate salvation from its effects and privileges. Do I undervalue the blood of Jesus, by seeking to *abound in hope through the power of the holy Ghost?* Do I the less trust in the Saviour's Righteousness, because *the Spirit itself beareth witness with my Spirit that I am a child of God, enabling me to cry abba Father?* Do I give the less credit to the written word, because I seek *to rejoice with joy unspeakable and full of Glory?* To have *access with boldness and confidence* is a fruit of divine faith. To be *sealed with the holy spirit of promise* is also the consequence of believing. And if *the love of God is shed abroad in my heart by the Holy Ghost* it is because I am *justified by faith*, and have peace with God through our Lord Jesus Christ.

I say therefore that there is much mischief done by telling God's people that they are to sit down contented without assurance and without comfort. These are the blessings which accompany Salvation, though not Salvation itself. These are the privileges of all true believers, though not the lot of all, especially at all seasons. Comfort and assurance must be sought in the use of the appointed means; they are incompatible with a careless, prayerless walk, or with the indulgence

of

of any one known sin, however small it may be thought. Whosoever would enjoy the consolations of the Spirit, must be afraid to grieve that blessed guest, or to quench his holy motions. The Christian, who most rejoiceth in the Lord, will be he who walks most humbly and most closely with his God.

Whoever would examine his comforts, to see from what source they are derived, would do well to pay attention to the following method of trial; for though hypocrites seldom suspect their comforts, yet the sincere soul will often be questioning the truth of them, and will be anxious to know from what fountain they flow.

First. If comforts proceed from Satan transformed into an Angel of light, they lead to sin and presumption; if from the Lord, they are always accompanied with a hatred of sin, (especially the sin which does most easily beset the soul) with a longing desire to obtain victory over it.

Secondly. The comforts which proceed from God are always accompanied with a spirit of prayer and of praise. A praying, thankful frame of mind is the very temper which a soul enjoying the sensible presence of its Saviour *naturally* (for the new nature has its actings as well as the old) falls into.—Whereas false comfort begets negligence in drawing near to God.

Thirdly.

Thirdly. Where comforts really proceed from the holy Ghost, they make Christ more and more precious in all his offices; and cause self to be abased, and to sink into nothing.—Whereas false comfort always puffeth up, and makes the soul think itself something when it is nothing.

No. XXXI.

IT may happen, that when a believer has been flattering himself that he has mastered all his corruptions, the old sore may break out again, and master him worse than ever, to his own grief and shame, and (if his falls be known) to the triumph of the Devil's children.

No. XXXII.

FAITH and Conversion are the manifestative evidences of that love which God had to his people from everlasting, and when they were dead in trespasses and sins. *Faith* is that messenger which brings to the soul the knowledge of its reconciliation with God, and union with Christ, and *Conversion* proves the truth of faith; *a great number*

number believed and turned unto the Lord. Acts xi. 21. No one grace can exist before Faith.—*Faith purifies the heart. Faith worketh by love. Faith overcometh the world.*

No. XXXIII.

THERE is a text in St. Paul's Epistle to the Ephesians, which loses much of its marrow and fatness as it is commonly taken and read. The words are these, Chap. ii. 4, 5. "But God, who is rich in mercy, for the great love wherewith he loved us even when we were dead in sins."

Thus the passage ought to be read; and here the stop ought to be put, and not where it usually is put, viz: after the words " hath quickened us together with Christ," which is a sort of tautology, and only shews an act of power, but by no means sets forth that act of free love to man as a sinner, yea in his sins, which the right sense of this scripture elucidates.

No. XXXIV.

THERE never was nor ever will be any variance between God and man but on account of sin.

sin. But sin is taken away by Chriſt, therefore thoſe who truly believe in him have no sin at all to anſwer for. The Law will often be charging sin on their conſciences, but Chriſt hath redeemed them from all its curſes. When they commit sin, they are apt to think, O now this sin is laid to my charge! God will impute it unto me, forgetting the Apoſtles challenge, *who ſhall lay any thing to the charge of Gods Elect?* and that *God was in Chriſt reconciling the world unto himſelf, not imputing their treſpaſſes unto them.* David does not ſay, *bleſſed is the man who has no sin,* he knew well that no ſuch man could have been found, but he ſays, *bleſſed is the man unto whom the Lord will not impute sin.*

No. XXXV.

TO a carnal man it muſt appear to be a very ſtrange diſſuaſive from sin, that though a believer commit sin, that sin which he commits ſhall not bring him under any condemnation, but that God the Father will be propitious and favourable to him on account of the advocacy of Chriſt: yet this is the very argument which the beloved diſciple makes uſe of, and every real chriſtian feels its force, to reſtrain from sin; for ſays he, *I write*

unto

unto you that you sin not, and if any man sin, we have an advocate with the Father, Jesus Christ the righteous; and he is the propitiation for our sins.

No. XXXVI.

There is not a moment in which every believer does not appear before God as pure and spotless as the blood of Christ can make him, yea as pure as the immaculate Lamb himself; nor is there a moment in which the holy law can find the smallest fault with him; seeing that the righteousness in which he stands, was as much wrought out by him in Christ, his second and spiritual head and representative, as the commandment was broken by him in Adam, his first and natural head and representative. The righteousness of Christ therefore is as much his, as the sin of Adam was his, and this righteousness always remains the same under all the various cases, states, and circumstances a believer can be in.

No. XXXVII.

THERE is not one gospel truth which nature doth not kick at with all her might. Even
awakened

awakened souls cannot receive them but as the Lord is pleased to teach them little by little in a way of Experience; and whoever gets them in any other manner had better be without them.— Nature knows nothing of any Religion but that of works —Even after the soul is married to Christ, she is hankering after her first husband the Law, and notwithstanding an Apostle tells her he is dead, she can hardly give full credit to him, though at the risk of being thought an Adulteress. Rom. vii. 2, 3, 4. Nay, there are some truths which nature kicks at with both legs, and she kicks contrary ways, till she even kicks herself in the face.

For Instance: when she hears of Salvation by faith only, the haughty dame kicks this away as licentious doctrine; but when she hears of vital holiness, and close walking with God, Oh! this she kicks at as unnecessary precisenes, and being righteous overmuch.

No. XXXVIII.

THERE are some ministers, who, if they have given their hearers a sip of pure gospel wine, and brought their souls into a glowing ardor, immediately

mediately throw a gallon of cold water upon them whereby all the flame is quenched, or to vary the metaphor (since the scripture makes use of both) (Isa. lv. 1.) if they have given them a taste of gospel milk, they cannot be satisfied till they have curdled it with a pailful of legal vinegar. Such ministers may mean well, but it wont do, the heart gets hard, guilt cankers the conscience, and the obedience which is produced, (if there be any at all) is at best slavish, never filial; they would guard against antinomianism, whilst in truth they produce it, by drawing the flaming sword of the Law, and thereby *guarding* the poor guilty sinners free approach to Christ the tree of life, from whom alone fruit unto holiness is to be found.

No. XXXIX.

DOES an Apostle say, "Pray without ceasing?" Then what a condition must those souls be in who never pray at all?—But what is meant by the exhortation? certainly it does not suppose that we should be always on our knees, yet it undoubtedly supposes that whatever be the posture of the body, the heart be constantly kept in a praying frame; and that *in every thing* we be ready to *give thanks*, or supplicate as circum-

stances

stances may require. I would boldly pronounce that man to be a stranger to the spirit of prayer, who confines it *merely* to times and places: for sure I am, that whosoever is made sensible of his own weakness, and of Christ's all-sufficiency, as well as of the continual blessings which he has received, is receiving, and hopes to receive from above, can never be long without a silent mental ejaculation at least, and such will find its way to the throne of grace, be the posture of the body what it may.

Every real christian knows well what it is to lift up his heart to God whilst he is walking, travelling, working, lying on his bed, and even when he is in company; and often is he holding an intercourse with Heaven, whilst those about him are busied only with the world.

Every believer's prayer must be answered, not always agreeably to his own wishes, but always in the way which shall be best for him.—When Paul had *the thorn in his flesh, the messenger of Satan sent to buffet him*, he prayed the Lord *thrice* that it might depart from him. But the Lord's answer was, " my Grace is sufficient for thee."

But a poor soul may say, Oh! prayer to me is all lip labour. I am only a speaking carcass before the Lord; I am wholly dead; I have no spirit of prayer; no access with boldness and confidence to the majesty on high. These very complaints are proofs, that thou knowest what no one but a believer can know, viz: the difference of addressing God from behind the cloud, and when he unveils his face, and shines with full lustre upon the soul. Press on then, though it be in the dark. Soon shall the sun of righteousness arise with healing under his wings.

XL.

SAINT PAUL says, *God was in Christ reconciling the world unto himself*, yea *that he hath reconciled us unto himself by Jesus Christ.* After which he adds: *we pray you in Christ's stead be ye reconciled to God*, 2 Cor. v. 18, 19, 20. But if reconciliation took place, when the God-head was in the manhood of Christ crucified, if the Church of Corinth was already pardoned and justified, why does he now beseech any, much less why does he intreat *believers* to be reconciled to God? Can they at the same time be reconciled and unreconciled? Is not this a contradiction.

There is no contradiction, but much beauty and more comfort in the passage. Although reconciliation, pardon and justification be one and only one compleat act, yet in scripture it bears a kind

kind of threefold afpect. *Firſt*, from all Eternity, as the elect were chofen in Chriſt from before the foundation of the world. *Secondly*, when Chriſt hung upon the crofs, and cried *it is finiſhed*. *Thirdly*, when the pardon and reconciliation which Chriſt hath obtained, are applied to the believing finner's heart and confcience by the Holy Ghoſt.—It is in this latter fenfe that thofe who already have reconciliation are prayed to be reconciled. And in the fame fenfe it is that our Lord teaches thofe to whom he has forgiven all trefpaffes, to pray " forgive us our trefpaffes as we forgive them that trefpafs againſt us :" fo that a believer is always reconciled, yea always perfectly reconciled, and not lefs fo at one time than another, as he may be apt to fuppofe, when his corruptions fhew their ugly gigantic heads : yet he ſtands in continual need of freſh applications of the blood of fprinkling to comfort his confcience, and to draw out his heart in a way of love and holy obedience.

XLI.

SANCTIFICATION is more to be judged of by inward workings of oppofition to fin, and longings after grace, than by any external acts

either

either good or bad. This is meant of a man's own judgment of himself; for as others cannot see the heart, they can judge only by outward actions.

No. XLII.

WHAT is the cause that the soul, which has been long converted, sometimes falls by the very sin which it seemed to have gotten a complete victory over? The plain simple reason is, that the soul is off its guard. Even the wise virgins, though they had oil in their lamps, all slumbered and slept.

The young convert in his battles against sin, is like a man fighting with a serpent, which he levels to the ground upon it's first attack, and so every time the venemous animal raises itself up against him, till the man leaves it, in his opinion, breathless upon the earth. But it soon appears, that the creature was only stunned, not killed; for recovering its force, it seizes the man unawares, and perhaps bites him worse than ever. Arise, my soul, and trim thy lamp, lest not sin only, but death surprise thee in a state of slumber.

No. XLIII.

No. XLIII.

THE moſt pure in heart, are uſually thoſe who moſt lament their heart impurity. It is by the light of grace only that the filthineſs of nature is diſcovered.

No. XLIV.

THOUGH a child of God glories in this, that *where ſin hath abounded, grace doth much more abound*; yet no child of God can ſin that grace may abound.

No. XLV.

WHENEVER Luther was aſked, what made the beſt Divine, he anſwered, *temptation*; and what makes the beſt Divine makes the beſt Chriſtian.

No. XLVI.

EVERY Child of God knows it to be found doctrine, that we are justified by faith only; and that true faith necessarily begets holiness and good works. Yet in the knowledge of this truth, many a gracious soul goes to work quite at the wrong end, and thereby loses both the privilege and comfort of looking directly at Christ as a sinner: by this means faith flags, and unbelief getting in, guilt and hardness fret and canker the conscience.—The soul in such a state reasons thus: "If victory over sin, if holiness and fruitfulness "be the certain evidences of faith, I fear I have "them not. I know well what I ought to be, "and what I would be; but alas! I am "such a poor, sinful, barren cumberer of the "ground, such an ungrateful backslider, that I "think the root of the matter is not in me." This is the usual language of grace (and true gracious language it is) behind the cloud. The man only who knows the law, sees how far he falls short of its demands: The scripture exhortations shew us more what we ought to be, than what any attain to. But try the secret workings of thy heart. Doest thou confent unto the law that it is good? Is fin thy grief and burden, and though it prevail again and again, doeft thou ftrive and pray againft it? doeft thou love thofe that are born of God? doeft thou try, at leaft, to clothe thyfelf with the whole armour of God? doeft thou relifh favory experimental preaching? doeft thou endeavour to fortify thyfelf under thy fore temptations by fuch promifes as thefe: *No weapon formed againft thee fhall profper. When thou paffeft through the fires, and through the waters, I will be with thee, &c. I will never leave thee, nor forfake thee. All things fhall work together for good to thofe who love God, to thofe who are the called after his purpofe?* And when thou prayeft, though thy prayer feem to be fhut out, and to meet with no anfwer, doeft thou ftrengthen thy plea by the examples of the Syro-phenician woman, the importunate widow, the deliverance of Peter out of prifon, the man who requefted the three loaves, and many other fcripture examples? Though thefe examples and thefe promifes may not all have occurred, yet they will be of fpecial ufe in time of need, and are recorded wholly that they may be fo.

If fuch be the workings of thy heart, be affured that they proceed from the blowings of the

fweet

sweet spirit of grace upon thy garden, which, though it may have many foul weeds in it, yet is not without its flowers; *the rose of Sharon, and lily of the valley* is there: and though the fruits and blossoms may be blown off by the nipping blasts of sin and temptation, yet there is life in the root, which will surely sprout out again, and endure unto everlasting life.

Look now at the heart or garden of the natural man, and however decent, formal and moral he may be, it will be just like the artificial flower-garden, which was exhibited at Westminster-bridge. It is only to be seen of men; beautiful without, in trees, flowers, and fruit; but the trees have no root, the flowers no scent nor fragrance, and the fruit is all hollow. As this garden, however, may look more fair to a beholder's eye than a real garden, so may the artificial, self-made christian appear to have fewer blemishes, more duties, and more outward works of righteousness, than the soul which is really God's husbandry—A man may do a great deal in religion from wrong ends and wrong motives; and where a placid natural disposition, with a freedom from temptations concur, he may be a famous Christian in his own eyes, and in the eyes of the world; but all this while, he may be an utter stranger to the faith of God's elect; his

heart

heart may be quite unrenewed, and all his fancied goodnefs, in God's fight, meer pride and felf-righteoufnefs, proceeding only from ignorance and felf-love.

No. XLVII.

WE fhould account him but an indifferent fhepherd who fhould lead his flocks to fandy deferts and muddled waters, whilft there were green paftures and clear ftreams at hand for their refrefhment. Yet there are fome minifters, who under the idea of being, what they call, *guarded*, are unwilling to truft God with his own truths, or to give his children their proper bread, for fear the dogs fhould fnap at it.

Moft certainly we cannot be too much on our guard againft fin, provided our weapons are taken from God's own arfenal. But fure it is, that whenfoever the gofpel is fo hafhed and cooked up that it becomes palatable to the tafte of human wifdom, it ceafes to be that gofpel which St. Paul preached.

Two objections efpecially were brought againft the doctrines of that apoftle. Thefe he ftates, and after giving them their full force, puts in his reply to each.

The

The first was against the doctrine of unconditional particular election, as making God cruel and unjust.

Objection. Thou wilt say then, why doth he yet find fault; for who hath resisted his will?

Answer. Nay, but O man, who art thou that repliest against God? Shall the thing formed say unto to him that formed it, why hath he made me thus? Hath not the potter power over the clay to make one vessel unto honor, another unto dishonor?

Objection. Is there unrighteousness with God?

Answer. God forbid; for how then should God judge the world?

The second objection was levelled against that grand pillar of a sinner's hope, justification by faith only, as if it were a doctrine tending to licentiousness, and to the overthrow of morality and good works.

This, the apostle says, some did not scruple to affirm; but he adds, that the report was slanderous. *Rom.* iii. 8.

Objection. Shall we sin then that grace may abound?

Answer. God forbid. How shall we that are dead to sin, live any longer therein?

Again. Objection. Do we then make void the law by faith?

Answer.

Anfwer. Nay, we eftablifh the law.

Now nothing can be more clear than that if I preach fuch doctrine as is not liable to thefe cavils of the objector, St. Paul's doctrine and mine are not one and the fame; and that we cannot both be in the right, is no lefs evident.

But the modern fyftem of divinity is not liable to thefe objections; on the contrary, modern divinity is the mother that nourifhes them againft the apoftle's doctrine : *Ergo*, either St. Paul's fyftem, or that of modern divinity, muft be grofsly erroneous.

No. XLVIII.

WHAT will that religion do for me that will not teach me to face death, and to meet that king of terrors with confidence ? As a finner, I am under condemnation ; but, as a believing finner, there is no condemnation for me. I am as much out of the reach of the law's curfe as if I had never broken it.—Sin can no more hurt me *(penally)* than if it had never entered into the world.—Death has no more fting for me, even when I pafs through it's dark vale, than it had for Adam in innocence. The grave has no more power over me than it had over Chrift himfelf.

(35)

Can this be true?—Read, believe, and suck the honey of these scriptures.

There is no condemnation to them that are in Christ Jesus. Christ hath redeemed us from the curse of the law, being made a curse for us.

He hath put away sin by the sacrifice of himself. He hath abolished death. Yea, he hath destroyed him that had the power of death, that is the Devil.

O death, I will be thy plagues. O grave! I will be thy destruction,—O death! where is thy sting? O grave where is thy victory?

The sting of death is sin, and the strength of sin is the law; but thanks be to God who giveth us the victory through our Lord Jesus Christ.

No. XLIX.

ALTHOUGH a believer may commit the same sins as an unbeliever, yea greater for the matter of them, as the cases of Lot, Sampson, David, Peter, the incestuous Corinthian, and others, do awfully evince; yet the believer's person, being screened from the curse of the law, cannot come under condemnation, even though the actings of repentance should be for a time suspended.

ed. But though his person cannot be arrested by the law, on account of Christ's having borne all the penalty due to the breach of it, yet is his sin equally displeasing to God; yea, much more so, as having been committed against light, grace, and love.

Though this consideration is of very great use to lift up a believer after a fall, it by no means affords him any encouragement to continue in sin; so far from it, that the more he sees of the pardoning love of Christ, so much the more odious will sin appear unto him. Whereas to *sin that grace may abound*, as it is the doctrine of hell, so none but Satan's first-rate pupils will ever adopt it.

L.

THE apostle bore this testimony to the believers of the church of Corinth, that they gave to the poor, not only to the utmost of their power, but *even beyond their power*. But there is a certain *close-fistedness* (if I may be allowed the expression) among too many professors of our day, who seem frightened out of their wits when any poor objects are recommended to their notice, insomuch that their niggardliness is even seen

through

through the muscles of the countenance, though they generally shelter their covetousness under the fear of giving amiss.—It is true, we are not to encourage idleness, and it well becomes us to see that our benevolence be not ill-placed; and yet I have frequently thought that if the Lord were to deal with us, and were to bestow his favors upon us only according to our deserts, the best of us would be very badly off indeed. But he is God and not man.

But Oh! the subterfuges which the avarice of the heart will fly too, whilst yet it is anxious to save appearances: " It is peculiarly inconvenient at this time." " Nobody knows how many calls I have lately had." Then a hint shall be thrown out, (with a seeming wish to conceal it) how much has been given upon other occasions.

After all, it is certain every man is best judge of his own abilities to give, as well as of the temper of his own heart in giving: therefore to his own master he must stand or fall. But let none be unmindful of the command given by one apostle, nor of the question put by another. *Do good unto all, especially to those who are of the houshold of faith.—If any man see his brother have need and shutteth up his bowels of compassion against him, how dwelleth the love of God in him?* In a word, we are stewards of all we possess, and the Lord will require an account of every talent committed to our charge. May grace enable us to use them aright!

LI.

THE key of prayer opens the gate of heaven, and there is not a state which a believer can be in, that there is not deliverance treasured up for him in Christ, which deliverance shall be given in the very moment that it is best for the believer it should be given. In the mean while, how earnestly will the soul plead with God! How will it search for scripture promises and scripture examples, and bring them to the throne of grace! though perhaps after all it will be saying " Surely there never was such a case as mine;" " never such a temptation as I am exercised with." Granted. Yet it must be included in the general promise; *there hath no temptation taken you but what is common to man; but God is faithful, who will not suffer you to be tempted above that you are able to bear, but will, with the temptation also, make a way for you to escape, that you may be able to bear it.*

" Oh! (says the soul) but this promise is come to an end with regard to me. I have fallen by the temptation; I have not been able to bear it; God hath not made a way for me to escape." Not perhaps by removing the temptation, nor by preserving thee altogether from being overcome by it;—still the promise is sure; and though thou may'st not escape a fall, yea many grievous foul falls, yet thou shalt certainly *escape ruin*; as the vessel which is tossed and battered by storms may still escape shipwreck. But remember that sincere prayer is absolutely incompatible with known sin, yea with any the least allowed evil. Far be it from me, however, to say that the soul who prays sincerely, may not be overcome by the very sin against which he prays; but this I say, that he cannot approve the sin by which he is overcome; his will cannot consent to it. *The evil that I would not, that I do,* is his language; and when victory over a bosom idol is given, he rejoices and is thankful.

No. LII.

IT is the distinguishing character of a believer, that he has fellowship with the Father and the Son, through the indwelling of the Spirit. Whosoever has not thus fellowship with God, hath fellowship with sin; and fellowship with God and fellowship with sin are incompatible. Yet a believer may have many sad falls into sin, without having fellowship with it. Grace and nature are inmates in the heart of a renewed man; yet they are just like two persons who dwell under the same roof, and are always at variance, they have no *fellowship* at all, the one with the other. The regenerate part *cannot sin, because it is born of God*; the divine seed remaineth in the believer uncorrupt and immaculate. *It is no more I, says the* apostle, *but sin which dwelleth in me.* Whereas *the carnal mind,* the unregenerate part *is not subject to the law of God, neither indeed can be.* On the contrary, *it is enmity against him.* It hates holiness, as being his image. It loves sin, and nothing but sin; sin is not only its law, but itself is *a law of sin* in the abstract. It is sleepless, restless, implacable, ever bent upon the ruin of the soul in which it dwells; and in the hour of temptation is particularly watchful to side with Satan, and to improve the advantage. Such a guest, rather such a desperate foe, does every believer carry in his bosom, which makes him so frequently cry out with St. Paul, *O wretched man that I am*; though at the very same time it is his privilege to exult with the same apostle and say, *I thank God, through Jesus Christ our Lord.*

No. LIII.

No. LIII.

THERE is not a believer in the world, who does not wish to have the government to remain in the Lord's hands, and who cannot at all times say, " thy will be done ;" I say *at all times*, for even at those seasons, when self-will is most at work, the believer wishes self to be dethroned, and acknowledges it to be right, that so it should be. Now sin directly strikes at the moral government of God, therefore in the very nature of things, sin and the believer must be at continual war ; and though the poor believer may get many a deep wound in his various battles against that cursed triple alliance, the world, the flesh and the devil ; (as often the bravest and most faithful soldier shall get the most bloody scars) yet the combat is sure to end gloriously, and he shall not only be conqueror, but *more than conqueror, through him that hath loved him.*

No. LIV.

A STATE of sin and a state of faith are directly opposite ; where sin reigns, unbelief is at the root; and where sin's dominion is broken, Christ dwells in the heart by faith: neverthelefs sin may reign where there is a very fine outside, and grace may reign where there is much corruption, yea, many out-breakings of it.

No. LV.

NOTHING tends to lay the soul so low as believing views of Christ; consequently so far is assurance from begetting pride, that the most assured Christian is the most humble Christian.

Nothing tends to promote holiness and good works but faith, therefore the Christian who has most assurance, will always be the most holy and the most fruitful Christian.

No LVI.

IT is the glory of the Gospel, that it sets the believer free from all condemnation, whether from the law, sin, death, hell or the grave: and that none of his transgressions, however great and aggravated, or whether before or after his conversion, shall ever be laid to his charge; seeing that they

were

were all laid upon Chrift in the everlafting covenant, and blotted out by him even before they were committed. Let thofe who would cavil at this affertion, firft try the truth of it; and let them confider how they will get peace to their troubled confciences any other way: perhaps there may come a time when they will be glad to embrace it. If they feek to obtain peace more or lefs in proportion as they keep or break the law, they are quite out of God's way of arriving at it, for he has ordained that peace fhall never come by *doing* but by *believing*; for *the law, as a miniftration of condemnation worketh wrath*; but, *being juftified by faith, we have peace with God, through our Lord Jefus Chrift*; and *the God of hope fills his people with joy and peace in believing*: but if the fins of all the elect were not laid upon Chrift at once, if they were not all blotted out at once, if they were not all pardoned at once (whether paft, prefent, or to come) how or when will they be taken away and pardoned? Is Chrift again to defcend from Heaven for this purpofe? Or, does he difpenfe his pardons, one by one, like the Pope of Rome?—The *knowledge* of forgivenefs of fins, it is true, is brought to the foul by believing; but pardon itfelf (at leaft the ground of pardon) is of the fame date with the grace and love of Jehovah to his people; It has no

depen-

dependance whatever on any thing in the creature, or that ever would be in the creature, whether of good to procure it, or of evil to prevent it. The motives of the eternal mind are in itself: *He order-eth all things after the counsel of his own will,* this will is immutable; it knoweth neither obstacle nor controul. *I will work, and who shall let? With him is no variableness, nor shadow of turning. I the Lord change not, therefore, the sons of Jacob are not consumed.*

When *the everlasting covenant* was planned between the three persons in the glorious and coequal Trinity, it was *ordered in all things and sure*; all the spiritual seed were then chosen in Christ their head, and grace was given them in him as members of his mystical body: all the sins that ever they should commit, with every aggravation with which they should be swelled, were taken into the account; payment was then *virtually* made, and, it was *actually* made when Jesus hung on the accursed tree; and all the powers of earth and hell combined can never charge one sin upon the soul for whom it was so paid and accepted: for *who shall lay any thing to the charge of God's elect?* Still the poor awakened sinner will be crying, " Oh! if I had not gone such lengths in sin; Oh! " if I had but turned a little sooner; Oh! if I had " not fallen so and so, I might then have hoped
" for

" for acceptance. But now I am so vile, surely
" the Lord will have no mercy on me."

How contrary is all this to God's method of Salvation, by Grace! but the Lord, in his due time, will beat the poor soul off from these legal self-righteous reasonings; and teach it *to live by the faith of the son of God, a life hid with Christ in God*; and this is the only way to be crucified unto the world, and to get victory over sin, and to make holiness the delight and element of the soul; nor can the believer have *access with boldness* to the throne of grace, but as he sees every impediment and bar to his approach, removed by Christ Jesus, and all his enemies under the feet of the captain of his salvation.

No. LVII.

MANY sincere souls are distressed because they think they have let the day of grace slip; these fears are good marks of that grace which they think they have not; but the idea itself has no foundation in scripture; for, *First*, reprobates have no day of grace, which, if improved, they would be saved; if neglected, they are lost. *Secondly*, the elect, however long they may have resisted, are assuredly brought to God in his own time, and in his own way; or, as the 17th article of the church of England, on *predeſtination and election*, well expreſſes it, *by his ſpirit working in due ſeaſon.* Their reſiſtance is no bar to the arm of omnipotence, nor can it for a moment retard *the time of love.*—*They* ſhall *be a willing people in the day of his power.*

No. LVIII.

SOME well-meaning miniſters of Chriſt are too apt to tell poor weak, toſſed, tempted chriſtians, that their doubts and fears are ſinful, and that they diſhonor God. This is *bruiſing the broken reed, and quenching the ſmoaking flame.* Unbelief is certainly a ſin, a ſtate of ſin, yea it is the ſin of ſins, for it is that which alone can damn the ſoul; but this is, by no means, the kind of unbelief that heavy leaden, afflicted ſouls complain of, and groan under, when convinced of ſin by the ſpirit, whoſe very doubts and fears evidence that they are in covenant with God, and have already *the faith of his own elect*, though they want ſuch a degree of it as to make them comfortable in their own conſciences; but if there was no faith, there would be no doubting, for theſe two are at once working in the heart, the one oppoſing the actings of the other,

other, so that my very fears that I have not faith, prove that I have it, as much as the bubblings and boiling of water in a furnace, prove the existence and the acting of the fire that is under it.

To say, that doubts and fears are sinful, is not the way to remove them, but to increase them, inasmuch as the sincere soul will fear more and more by thinking it has more sin to answer for: Besides, did any christian ever arrive at the sunshine of solid peace and assurance, but through clouds of doubts and fears? Tell me, ye that give vinegar and gall to bruised souls, by representing their doubts and fears, as adding to their guilt; did our Blessed Saviour ever hold this language? view him all the while he was upon earth, and you shall never hear him speak a discouraging word to the weak in faith, but always the contrary.

Lastly. If doubts and fears are traced to their origin, no culpable unbelief, no consent of the will will ever be found at the bottom of them, but real faith will always be discovered at their root; for why does the soul fear at all? but because it believes the truth of God's word, as threatning punishment and condemnation on account of its transgressions of the law. And why does the soul doubt?—Not because it disbelieves the promises therein contained; but,

because

because seeing its own sin and depravity, and God's holiness and purity, and not having clear views of the Lord's method of justifying the ungodly, without money, and without price, it distresses and perplexes itself, with the notion, that its great vileness is a bar to the mercy of God. Nature must, in a manner, be reversed, and turned topsy turvy before this great scriptural truth will be received, viz: that *sin, not goodness, qualifies every person for the Gospel Salvation.*

The verity of the promises then is not questioned by the feeble doubting Christian; but what he doubts and fears is, that he himself has no interest in them; and so far is Christ from being displeased with such weaklings, that his bowels yearn with a more than common tenderness over them; as a good shepherd, *he carries such lambs in his bosom, and gently leads those that are with young.*

Is this pleading for unbelief? Is it apologizing for doubts and fears? By no means: but the plea or apology is for that grain of true faith, which, like a living spark in the ashes, often lies smothered under the clog of unbelief, and under the weight of many suspicions and misgivings as to its state Godwards.—*Lord I believe, help thou mine unbelief*, should be the Christian's cry in such a state.

No. LIX.

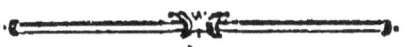

No. LIX.

EVERY believer generally fees in the courfe of his experience, that thofe very trials or temptations which he moft feared, and perhaps which he moft prayed againft, are thofe very bleffings in God's over-ruling hand, which he will be thankful for throughout eternity.

No. LX.

IT is not to be wondered that Hazael, who knew nothing of his own heart, fhould fay, "Is thy fervant a dog that he fhould do this thing;" but the felf-confidence of Peter was extraordinary, when he faid " Lord though all men fhall deny thee, yet will not I." Oh how little do many of the Lord's deareft people know what will befall them before they reach the end of their pilgrimage! When temptation is at a diftance, and all goes on fmoothly, we are too apt to think more highly of ourfelves than we ought to think; but let a ftrong temptation work upon a fuitable corruption in the heart, (Satan and opportunity blowing up the flame,) and there is no saying what may happen. It was well obſerved by that evangelical divine, Mr. John Hill, that "heed ought to be taken by the beſt of ſaints againſt the worſt of ſins." *Watch and pray* therefore *that ye enter not into temptation.* And *let him that thinketh he ſtandeth take heed leſt he fall.* But if thou haſt fallen, let not thy ſin drive thee to deſpair, but to Chriſt, that thou may'ſt be delivered both from its guilt and power.

LXI.

I HAVE often been grieved to perceive ſo very little of the chriſtian ſpirit and temper in many perſons, of whoſe converſion we cannot well doubt. Envy, malice, hatred, uncharitableneſs, evil ſurmiſings, ſwellings, whiſperings, backbitings, &c. are ranked by inſpiration itſelf, in the catalogue of the fouleſt offences; and yet we often ſee ſoaring profeſſors too much, alas! under the power of theſe evils, ſitting in judgment perhaps upon a poor fallen believer, who may have been overtaken with a fault, or raſhly cenſuring their brethren, even for things in themſelves indifferent.

It

It would be well if such persons would read the 13th chapter of St. Paul's first epistle to the Corinthians, and ask themselves, Have I this divine grace of charity or love, which envieth not, which thinketh no evil, which is not easily provoked, which vaunteth not herself, which seeketh not her own, which is not puffed up, but like the wisdom which cometh from above, is gentle and easy to be intreated? Without this I am nothing but sounding brass, or a tinkling cymbal.

Lord, evermore give me this grace! O let me be much at home! Let me search and ransack every corner of my deceitful heart, lest after all my profession, I fall short and come to nothing.

O my soul, is this thy prayer? yea, is it thy earnest wish and endeavor to know, feel and experience the full extent of the apostle's words, when he says, *now abideth these three, faith, hope and charity; but the greatest of these is charity!*

Still, under a mistaken notion of charity, I am not to put out my eyes, and to call evil good, and good evil. But I am to judge favorably whenever I can; and I am also to remember that he who stands to-day may fall to-morrow, and that who falls to-day may rise to-morrow.

No. LXII.

WHEN an impertinent, troublesome visiter knocks at the door and craves admission, the good man of the house usually denies himself. He is not at home to such company: the fellow may go about his business.

So should the believer always deal with sin when it stands knocking at the door of the heart. He must not begin parlying, but give it a flat denial: he must be at home to no such guest. To stand and argue is to let it halfway in.

But when Jesus knocks and says "Open to me, my beloved," it must be just the contrary.

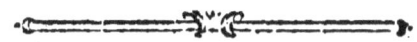

No. LXIII.

THERE is no time of a believer's experience in which he does not look upon sin as the greatest evil, and God as his greatest good. Even in the moment that he is so overborne by temptation as to choose the evil and refuse the good, still his judgment is not changed; and he says "the good that I would, I do not, but the evil which I would not, that I do."

No. LXIV.

No. LXIV.

THERE are those who cry out, "O I don't trouble myself about abstruse and disputed points of doctrine, give me our Saviour's sermon upon the mount!" yet bring them to the test of this sermon, and you will hear them call poverty of spirit, meanness; mourning for sin, folly and weakness; hungering and thirsting after righteousness, enthusiasm and being righteous overmuch; yea they will tell you that all persecution for righteousness sake was confined to primitive times; and that it is uncharitable to affirm that strait is the gate and narrow is the way that leadeth unto life, and that there are but few that find it.

No. LXV.

THOSE persons and those things which we have made our idols, God very frequently makes our plagues and our crosses.

No. LXVI.

WHOSOEVER knows what sin is, and what Christ is, that man is wise in God's account, whatsoever else he may be ignorant of.

Whosoever knows not himself as a sinner, nor Christ as a Savior, is a fool in God's account, whatever else he may be acquainted with, and however wise he may be in the world's estimation. No human science can teach a soul the evil of sin. Nor can all the learning in the world comfort a distressed conscience.

No. LXVII.

WATCHFULNESS will not avail without prayer, nor prayer without watchfulness. *Watch* and *pray*, saith our Lord.

No. LXVIII.

IT is a good observation of the worthy Doctor Fuller, in his Church History, that "those are the best Christians who are more careful to reform themselves than to censure others."

It is however a small thing to be judged of man's judgment. The world, it must be expected, will be void of charity towards God's people, and judge them as fools, hypocrites, enthusiasts, evil-designing, turbulent persons, and what not; but it is much to be lamented that the children of grace should judge one another so rashly as we often see them do: and this unhappy
spirit

spirit of censure is very apt to vent itself from persons in a lower station of life towards those whom it may have pleased God to place in a situation and sphere of life quite different from or above their own, which renders them very incompetent judges of those things of which they set themselves up to be censurers. I would not say that envy or spiritual pride, nor even a narrow, illiberal way of thinking are always the parents of this temper; I have seen it in honest simple-hearted souls, who are too apt to run away with appearances without examining things to the bottom; and I know how to make allowances for it: however, if such persons would turn their eyes within, they would there perhaps find much more cause for humiliation and condemnation than there is in a chearful countenance, or in living according to the rank and station which a gracious and wise Providence has appointed us; by which means multitudes are supported, employed and kept from idleness, who otherwise must steal, starve, or become burdensome to parishes.

But let those highly favoured few among the great or rich, whom grace has distinguished from others, always remember 1*st*. That the use of abundance, without the abuse of it, is an hard but needful lesson. 2*dly*. That sin in any station is alike displeasing to God. And 3*dly*. That he who

ventures

ventures to the utmost brink of his liberty, will be in danger of going beyond it. *Let their moderation therefore be known unto all men.* Let them remember too, that though feeding the hungry, clothing the naked, visiting the sick, and employing the poor to work, are distinguishing branches of real charity, yet that the cause of Christ, and the faithful ministers of the gospel, (especially those with scanty pay and large families) have the first claim on their abundance: and that although in cases of public charities our works must needs be seen before men, and indeed ought to be so, yet here there is no occasion that even the left hand should know what the right hand doeth, much less should it be blazoned abroad in the world: seasonable donations to poor godly labourers in the Lord's vineyard (and truly such are commonly *poor* enough) especially when those donations come unexpected, are often received as boons from above, and indeed are so when given for the gospel's sake, and shall in no wise lose their reward.

Here then a Christian may be often doing that very liberally, which an uncharitable professor may be censuring him for not doing at all. But God knoweth the heart, and knoweth all things.

I say therefore both to high and low, to rich and poor: *Judge not that ye be not judged.*

Rather

Rather put on that *charity* which *hopeth all things*, and which *thinketh no evil.*

Lord, evermore give thy children this temper one towards another.

No. LXIX.

A TRUE Saint may be a grievous backflider in practice, but he cannot be a backflider in principle. He would do good according to the law in his mind, even when evil is prefent with him through the law of fin which is in his members: but the force of corruption is fo violent, that he is brought into captivity to that law of fin, and by its tyranny holden down in fpight of all his groans and ftruggles for deliverance, which however in the ufe of the appointed means he fhall moft affuredly obtain in the Lord's own time. Yea, *though a troop may overcome him* (like Gad) *he fhall overcome at the laft.*

It is not fo with the backflider in heart. His falls into fin caufe him to depart from the appearances he might have of grace, till at at laft he falls from all profeffion. The fin that he commits he even approves in his heart, though natural confcience, till quite feared, may at times give him fome uneafy fenfations. All his falls into fin drive him further and further from God, whereas thofe of true believers

believers caufe them to flee to Chrift for ftrength, and to walk more warily for the future.

No. LXX.

TO a believing foul there is fomething wonderfully fweet in viewing all his trials, troubles, afflictions, temptations, defertions, fpiritual conflicts, ups and downs of every kind as ordered of God for his good; decreed to come upon him juft at fuch a time and place as his heavenly father's wifdom fees fit and meet; to remain with him juft fo long and not a fingle moment longer than till they fhall have anfwered fome falutary purpofe for his foul's good; that however fore and grievous thefe things may be to flefh and blood, however thwarting to his own will and wifhes, yea however contrary to what he would judge to be for his fpiritual welfare; yet he who ordereth all things after the counfel of his own will, caufeth them to work together for his good, and that they are all the effects and emanations of infinite wifdom, infinite love, and infinite power united to accomplifh his falvation in the way that fhall be beft for him, and moft for his heavenly father's glory.

No. LXXI.

No. LXXI.

THE scripture hath given seven reasons (which in the sacred writings is a perfect and compleat number) for the practice of good works. Yet such is the pride and ignorance of man that he will needs add *an eighth*, though this eighth reason turns all good works into bad ones, impeaches God's wisdom, and makes the blood of Christ of none effect.

The scripture reasons for the performance of good works are the following:

1.

THEY are commanded by God himself.—Tit. iii. 8. This is a faithful saying, and these things I will that thou affirm constantly, that they which have believed in God might be careful to maintain good works.

2.

God's people are predestinated, chosen and born again in Christ Jesus for this very purpose.—Eph. ii. 10. We are his workmanship, created anew in Christ Jesus unto good works, which God hath before ordained that we should walk in them.

3. Good

3.

Good works are the external evidences of true living faith here, and will be so at the day of judgment; according to which a reward of grace will be given. Faith, if it hath not works, is dead, being alone.—I will shew thee my faith by my works. Jam. ii. 17, 18, &c. For the Son of Man shall come in the glory of his Father, with his angels; and then shall he reward every man according to his works. Mat. xvi 27.

See also Mat. xxv. from v. 31 to the end of the chapter.

4.

The love of Christ to us as sinners excites us to the practice of them, yea to be *zealous* for them.

2 Cor. v. 14. For the love of Christ constraineth us.

John, xvi. 15. If ye love me, keep my commandments.

Tit. ii. 14. He gave himself for us to purify to himself a peculiar people zealous of good works.

5.

The example of Christ and his apostles teacheth and enforceth them.

Acts,

Acts, x. 38. Jesus of Nazareth went about doing good.

1 Cor. xi. 1. Be ye followers of me, even as I also am of Christ.

6.

When performed from right motives and to right ends, they tend to glorify God.

Mat. v. 16. Let your light so shine before men that they may see your good works, and glorify your Father which is in heaven.

7

They are for the profit and advantage of our fellow creatures, and of our fellow Christians.

Gal. vi. 10. Do good unto all, especially to those who are of the household of faith.

Tit. iii. 8. These things (good works) are good and profitable unto men.—See also Jam. ii. 14, 15, 16.

1 John iii. 17. Whoso hath this world's good, and seeth his brother have need, how dwelleth the love of God in him?

These are the scripture reasons for the practice of good works, yet vain man who would set up to be wiser than his maker, would be thrusting in another use for good works which he thinks preferable to all the rest, though in fact it tends to

F subvert

subvert and defeat the whole gospel plan of salvation, *namely*, to recommend us to the favor of God, either in whole or in part, or at least to serve as conditions of our justification and acceptance. Thus teach all the Papists. Thus teach too many who are called Protestants, in direct opposition to the word of God, and to the confessions of all the reformed churches, particulary to the 9th, 10th, 11th, 12th, and 13th articles of the church of England.

No. LXXII.

IN order that no poor convinced sinner may despair of mercy, there is no sin that ever was, or can be commited (the sin against the Holy Ghost excepted, which none have committed who are willing to be saved in the gospel way) which some that are now in glory have not been guilty of. Murderers, adulterers, incestuous persons, abusers of themselves with mankind, drunkards thieves, extortioners, revilers and deniers of Christ, swell the list of those who are washed, sanctified and justified in the name of our Lord Jesus, and by the spirit of our God.

Nay more, there is perhaps not a sin which can be thought of, that some of God's eminent

scripture

scripture saints have not fallen into after their conversion, though through grace they have been enabled to renew the actings of their faith and repentance, and are now singing before the throne " unto him that hath loved and redeemed them, and that hath washed them from their sins in his own blood."

And for fear any should still object against themselves, " oh but my sins are of such a nature, that surely no saved soul was ever guilty of the like;" our Lord himself says that *all manner of sin and wickedness shall be forgiven.* And the beloved John assures us that *the blood of Jesus Christ cleanseth from all sin.*

Now let the whole self-righteous tribe of formalists murmur at these glorious displays of invincible grace, as their forefather Simon the Pharisee did of old, when the poor, sinful, penitent Mary washed our Savior's feet with her tears, and wiped them with the hairs of her head; still it must ever stand upon record, that the debtor to whom five hundred pence was forgiven, loved more than he did to whom only fifty pence was forgiven; and that publicans and harlots go into the kingdom of heaven before the generation of those who are pure in their own eyes, and yet are not cleansed from their filthiness.

No. LXXIII.

MANY sincere souls, who are truly converted to God, are apt to think that surely persons who have run such lengths in sin as they have, ought never to expect the same degrees of sensible comfort and communion with God, as others may enjoy, who have not resisted so many calls of love, nor sinned with so high an hand as themselves; especially if they have been notorious backsliders, although now through grace renewed again unto repentance, are they apt to cherish these legal reasonings, so contrary to the whole gospel plan, so derogatory to the honor of Christ, and so destructive to the soul's peace. Their language is just this:

Had I owed only fifty pence, Jesus would have forgiven me more *frankly*, and I might have expected more manifestations of his love than I can hope for, who am a poor five hundred pence debtor, and who have nothing at all to pay." Again: " I have contracted great and heavy debts since my conversion. I am a grievous backslider; and though I now desire to repent of my sins, and turn to the Lord with all my heart, I fear he will not receive me graciously. At least, if

he

he does restore me to his favor, I must go halting, and walk in darkness all my days, without ever feeling his sweet sensible presence in my soul." Alas, poor creature! has the Lord said that he is married to his backsliding children, and doth he urge his relationship of an husband to them as the motive of their return to him; (Jer. iii. 14.) and will he not receive them when they do return? Has he promised to *heal their backslidings, and to love them freely?* (Hosea, xiv. 4.) and will he be worse than his word? Has he told us to forgive a repenting brother not only until seven times, but until seventy times seven; and will he who is God, and not man, do less? Did the long forsaken father fall upon the returning prodigal son's neck and kiss him; and will not thy heavenly Father and bridegroom, whose compassions are infinite, embrace thee in the arms of his love, and *kiss thee with the kisses of his mouth?* Cant. i. 2.—ii. 6. Yea, he will, he will. Seek him then, though thick dark clouds of desertion, and though mountains of sin and corruption would impede thy way. Seek him in the use of all means, yet trusting to none.

  Whate'er's thy husband at thy best,
   He's at thy worst the same:
  And in his love will ever rest,
   Jehovah is his name.

GOSPEL SONNETS.
LXXIV.

No. LXXIV.

SIN is the the disease of the renewed soul; but it is the element of the natural man.

No. LXXV.

THOUGH Christ has reconciled sinners to himself, yet it is absolutely impossible for any Christian to be reconciled to sin.

No. LXXVI.

IT is not possible for a believer to be contented with his present attainments. It is the grand proof of a renewed mind that it fights vigorously against all sin inward as well as outward, that it desires, yea pants to grow in grace and in the knowledge of our Lord and Savior Jesus Christ; that it hungers and thirsts after righteousness; that it longs to lay itself out for the glory of God, and to abound more and more in every good word and work.

Where this is not the cafe, faith is not: and where faith is not, Chrift is not; and where Chrift is not, Satan muft be.

No. LXXVII.

WHEN God elected his people in Chrift and reconciled them to himfelf in him, he forefaw all the evil that would be in them both before and after their converfion; and if this did not prevent his choofing them and calling them, it never can be the caufe of his cafting them off.

No. LXXVIII.

THOUGH affurance be the privilege of all God's people, it is by no means the lot of all. Neverthelefs it is the duty of all to prefs after it.

Affurance is the higheft degree of faith, and faith being the root of holinefs, as faith prevails holinefs and deadnefs to the world will prevail; for this is the victory that overcometh the world, even our faith.

Peter's affurance gave way, and he fell foully. But Chrift prayed that his faith might not fail, and he fell not finally.

If,

If, as some affirm, assurance begets a careless walk, then the most desirable state a Christian can be in would be that of despair, as being the direct opposite to assurance; and the prayer of the apostles "Lord increase our faith," should be turned into "Lord increase our unbelief, and diminish our faith," lest it grow into assurance, and we should thereby be emboldened to commit iniquity with greediness."

But the soul that really enjoys assurance knows how to prize that precious jewel, and will walk as humbly and as warily, as he who being clearly and richly attired would pick his way upon a plank over some dirty road, lest he should slip aside, and defile his garments.

No. LXXIX.

THE dead sinner partakes of two natures; or at least of two parts of one nature. Half beast, half devil.

The glorified saint partakes only of one nature, viz. the divine.

A regenerate believer partakes of all the three; but though the remnants of the beast and devil are yet in him, he is denominated by that which bears the rule and ascendency; and therefore the apostle

apoſtle addreſſes ſuch as being _partakers of the divine nature_ only.

No. LXXX.

IT is one of the firſt and cleareſt truths in the Bible that a believer hates ſin, and becauſe he hates ſin, he muſt love the law. But it is no leſs true, that the moſt advanced believer knows, feels and laments that he loves ſin, and that he continually carries that about with him which is not ſubject to the law of God, neither indeed can be.

It is not ſcriptural to ſay that he hates ſin ſo far as he is regenerate, though the phraſe be a common one: that expreſſion _ſo far_ ſeems rather to imply an amendment of _the old man_ than a _putting on the new._ The truth is, that every believer has a perfect old nature, and a perfect new nature, both fighting together within him. When he commits ſin, it is not becauſe his new nature is not yet compleat, nor becauſe his old nature is but in part deſtroyed, but becauſe the old man is forever reſtleſs, and ſtriving to recover the entire maſtery he once had over the believer: but in the end he muſt yield, and even now though he never ceaſes to fight, yet he never gains the dominion.

minion. The renewed will is an impregnable caſtle which almighty grace enables to hold out againſt the combined aſſaults of ſin, Satan and the world. The believer then is always compleatly holy in his new nature, for God's workmanſhip muſt be perfect. He is compleatly unholy in his old nature, for *in him, that in his fleſh there dwelleth no good thing.* Theſe two are waging perpetual war in the ſoul, ſeeing what the one loves the other hates, and *vice versâ.* But the law of grace muſt finally triumph over the law of ſin: during this deſperate combat, all the believer's confidence is in Chriſt, in whom he is always compleat, and in whom he has ſuch a righteouſ‑ neſs, as neither the law, ſin, death, hell or the grave can fully or find fault with.

No. LXXXI.

THE man that has leaſt ſin has not always moſt grace. Great grace is uſually given to fight againſt great corruptions. Few have known more ſin or more grace than David.

No. XCII.

No. LXXXII.

ST. PAUL, like a wise master-builder, having laid the foundation of a guilty sinner's hope on Christ alone, raises thereon the superstructure of holiness and walking with God; and, at the close of his epistles, gives the warmest exhortations to the practice of every relative and social duty: it has therefore often been matter of astonishment to me to behold so many golden, or perhaps I ought rather to say *gilded* professors paying so little attention to these exhortations. One has very unsubdued tempers; another is a rigid cruel parent; a third is a stubborn undutiful child; a fourth is a surly Nabal of an husband; a fifth an idle, gossiping, tatling wife; a sixth an hard tyrannical master or peevish mistress, never pleased and always changing his or her servants; a seventh is a negligent, wasteful, eye servant, saucy, pert answering again, running about from one professor to another to carry about family news, and to expose the real and imaginary faults of those with whom they live. Lastly, and which is worst of all, an eighth, is a minister that ought never to be seen but in the pulpit.

Oh, my soul, how grievous, and yet how common

mon are thefe things! furely fuch perfons have much reafon to queftion the reality of their converfion, fince lying, ftealing, fabbath-breaking, and all manner of profanenefs cannot be more oppofite to the true fpirit of Chriftianity than fuch difpofitions and fuch practices. I know indeed it is too much the manner of fome to run down all exhortations to obedience and to holy walking as legal, but I would always wifh to proclaim as on the houfe top, that he only who liveth near to God and keepeth his confcience tender and void of offence, has any folid proof of his intereft in Chrift; and that the man who is not watchful in life, has awful reafon to tremble at the approach of death, left the hope with which he has buoyed himfelf up, (perhaps under a towering profeffion, and a critical knowledge of gofpel doctrines,) fhould after all turn out only the hope of the hypocrite which fhall perifh.

No. LXXXIII.

WHEN a believer reads the character of a true Chriftian in the facred pages, he fees his own fhort comings in every grace; and is deeply humbled under the fenfe of them.—This is right. But

he

he should remember that the scripture exhortations rather call believers to what they ought to be than what any arrive to. There can be no rule of right or wrong but the will of God; therefore, when believers are excited to holiness, it must be to that which is perfect, else the law immediately gives way to the frailty of the creature. The language of scripture is in this wise, *be ye holy, for I am holy: be perfect as your Father which is in heaven is perfect*. And indeed it could not be otherwise, without running in the following strain, which it would be almost blasphemous to suppose; " be ye a little holy and a little sinful:" " be like your Father which is in heaven, but not too like."

Hence we see the absurdity and impiety of what some call *a remedial law of grace*. We see also that a believer in view of his imperfections and short comings, will at once find cause both for humiliation and for consolation; for *humiliation*, in that he feels that sin cleaves to, and poisons all his best actions; the flesh lusteth against the spirit, and the spirit against the flesh, so that he cannot do the things that he would; and his language in his best state must be, *not as though I had already attained, or were already perfect*. For *consolation*, in that God views him more according to what he would be, than what he is; and that though he is nothing but sin and imperfection in himself, he is always compleat in Christ, who of God is made unto him wisdom, righteousness, sanctification and redemption.

No. LXXXIV.

THE true meaning of the word repentance is a change of mind; and how can this be accomplished without faith? and how can faith exist without justification? Genuine repentance then with its meet fruits flowing from Christ, and being the effect of the soul's union with and interest in him, is the certain proof that the soul has received mercy, though neither repentance nor any other grace, but, on the contrary, only sinfulness, fits and prepares for mercy. To place repentance before reconciliation, or to affirm that it is preparatory thereto, is (as already noticed) to put the effect before the cause, and to look for fruit on the tree before it is either planted or ingrafted. It is moreover to establish the Romish doctrine of grace of congruity, which our Reformers, in the 13th article of religion, have so expresly borne their testimony against. Indeed it is to preach another gospel than what Paul preached. Yet it is amazing how incautiously some pious and good

men

men have expressed themselves on this point. Again. Repentance, being a change of mind, cannot be eradicated from the believer by any falls into sin, since the renewed mind hates the sin which the believer falls into. His state God-ward is not affected by his falls, though his peace will be much affected; seeing he as much is out of his proper element under the prevalence and out-breakings of corruption, as a fish would be out of its element if you were to take it out of the sea and lay it in the sun-beams: the poor fish jumps and flounders about, and is wretched till it get into the water again; so will the poor fallen believer strive and struggle hard till he finds himself brought into his own element, which is holiness. An animal, whose nature is cleanly, a sheep for instance, may undoubtedly fall into the mire; but a sheep cannot delight himself in the mire into which he falls, but will pant, bleat and struggle till the shepherd come and help him out. One of Christ's sheep may fall foully into dirt and filth, but the cleanly nature will shew itself by incessant cryings and exertions till deliverance be obtained.

It is not so with a swine. Its nature being filthy, it delights in filth; and though you may wash it again and again, it has no real enjoyment but what it finds in mud and nastiness.—This is just the case with every natural man.

It may be objected that repentance in fcripture is put before faith "Repent ye and believe the gofpel." But when both are neceffary, the order in which they are mentioned is no proof at all which of thefe bleffings firft takes place in the foul. Sanctification is mentioned by St. Paul previous to juftification, " but ye are fanctified, ye are juftified;"* yet no one (I mean none but a blind Formalift, or a Papift) will affirm that any foul is made holy before it has pardon through blood of Chrift. In like manner, in the Revelation, calling is placed before choice, " called and chofen;" yet every Chriftian knows that we are called becaufe we are elected, and not called firft and elected afterwards.

But whenever the fcripture fpeaks of repentance as a turning of the heart to God, then it is always placed fubfequent to faith " Many believed and turned to the Lord." By faith in the exceeding great and precious promifes, we are made partakers of a divine nature. However, if we confider repentance in a double point of view, viz. as legal and evangelical, it will readily be granted that the firft of thefe, which is more properly attrition than contrition, precedes faith, or rather the foul's own knowledge of faith, for there muft

---

* 1 Cor. vi. 11. See alfo 2 Theff. ii. 13. Where fanctification of the Spirit is placed before belief of the truth.

be

be a degree of faith to put the foul on flight to Chrift. But true, ingenuous, melting repentance is the fruit of advanced faith; and even the higher the foul rifes towards full unclouded affurance, and towards that love that cafteth out fear, fo much the more genuine will its humiliations be on account of fin.

No. LXXXV.

IF the whole body of the elect were chofen in Chrift from eternity, and if grace was given them in him before the foundations of the world, then all the fpiritual feed muft have been confidered as members of Chrift, the fecond Adam, and one with him, when the eternal counfel of peace was made with him their glorious head, (as much as they were confidered in Adam at the time of his apoftacy in Paradife;) and every bleffing which they fhould enjoy in time, was then made fure to all the feed, without any refpect to good or evil in them; or whether viewed in the pure or in the corrupt mafs, which feems a needlefs diftinction, though much contefted by fome great and good men, feeing all things are prefent with the eternal mind of Jehovah: and every event which concerns God's Church and people from the creation of the world to the end of it, even that

that greatest of all transactions, the crucifixion of Christ, is but the manifestation of the glory of that wonderful covenant, which is ordered in all things and sure; and which will have its final accomplishment when the number of the elect shall be called in, and every member of the church militant join those of the church triumphant in singing "Worthy is the Lamb," &c. &c.

No. LXXXVI.

THE belief of final perseverance is an excellent spur to make a believer humble, holy, active, as well as to raise him up after falls and backslidings, and this upon the apostolic principle, *knowing that his labor shall not be in vain in the Lord.*—Whereas the man who knows himself, and sees the strength of his enemies, would lie down and despair if he did not believe the promise that *he who hath begun the good work in him will perfect it unto the day of Jesus Christ.*

No. LXXXVII.

IT frequently happens that when a child of God has experienced the sweetness of any promise, or seen and tasted something of the glory

of

of Chrift in any particular text of fcripture, that afterwards he will be turning to the fame promife, or to the fame portion of holy writ, the tafte of which he had found fo precious to his foul; but alas! the favour may be evaporated, and he him-. felf may have no more relifh for what he fo lately, found as honey and the honeycomb. Now what is the reafon of this, fince the promife is the fame; Chrift is the fame; and the believer's intereft in, both is always the fame?—It is certainly owing to the fovereignty of God *the Spirit, who bloweth when and where he lifteth.*

No. LXXXVIII.

PARDON of fin is one thing; knowledge of pardon another. The foul that under a fenfe of guilt applies itfelf to the Redeemer for mercy is furely already pardoned. Such an one is reconciled to God by virtue of the everlafting covenant. This pardon and reconciliation though eternal and immutable by that covenant, was ratified when Jefus hung on the crofs, and it is paffed over to the finner in his fins, and *in his blood*, whilft he is an *enemy* and *ungodly*, *rebellious* and *without ftrength*, confequently whilft he is an unbeliever; but the knowledge of this is often for a long while

while with-holden from the foul, yea there may be thofe *who all their lifetime are fubject to bondage,* and yet fhall get fafe home at laft. Though the covenant be *ordered in all things and fure*, yea as fure as the immutable oath and promife of God can make it, *to all the elect feed* of grace, yet in order that God's faints may know the value of it, they are all made to feel *the plague of their own hearts,* and the bitternefs of fin: they are therefore made *weary and heavy ladin* by the *fpirit of bondage to fear,* before they receive the *jpirit of adoption,* manifefting to them the relationfhip in which they ftand as reconciled finners, and enabling them to cry *Abba Father.*

The Law as a miniftration of condemnation, muft do its office on the foul before it will welcome the gofpel as glad tidings, and clofe with it as a covenant of free grace and peace, and therefore the prince of peace bears this record of himfelf. *The fpirit of the Lord is upon me, becaufe he hath anointed me to preach the gofpel to the poor, he hath fent me to heal the broken-hearted, to preach deliverance to the captives, and recovering of fight to the blind, to fet at liberty them that are bruifed.*

No. LXXXIX.

No. LXXXIX.

SOULS under saving awakenings and convictions of sin have no idea how much legality, self-righteousness and cleaving to the law of works is in them; nay, though they will acknowledge salvation to be by faith only in Christ and though they attend clear gospel preaching, yet they are apt to reason thus with themselves; "Oh that I "had not gone such lengths in sin! Oh that I "had but taken up sooner! Oh if I had not re- "belled so much against light and conscience and "solemn resolutions to the contrary! If my "transgressions were not of such and such a na- "ture, I could then venture to believe in Christ "for pardon and salvation; but now I fear he "will cast me out if I come unto him." According to all this reasoning <u>Moses not Christ has the pre-eminence</u>, and in truth it all comes to this issue, "<u>God will be favorable to me or not in proportion as I have kept or broken the law.</u>" But though Pharisees should rage and formalists should storm at the blessed truth, yet it is the glorious declaration of the gospel, that the man who has gone as far as sin can go to his damnation, has not gone so far as Christ can go, or rather *has gone*, for his

salva-

salvation: [see Rom. v. throughout.] And though one single offence and that only in thought will shut up the soul under condemnation without the blood of Christ, yet whosoever flies as a perishing sinner to that precious *fountain opened for sin and for uncleanness, though his sins be as scarlet, they shall be as wool; though they be red like crimson, they shall be white as snow.*

It is certain that no man can ever view sin in too detestable a light; but if he views it in such a manner as to eclipse his views of Christ, he cannot feel any kindly ingenuous sorrow on account of it. Sin viewed in the law begets terror and hardness. Viewed in the gospel it begets sweet relentings of soul.

No. XC.

EVERY believer is sanctified in a two-fold sense.

1*st*. In himself, by the mortification of sin, and by the renewal of his soul in holiness, after the image of God. This sanctification is often sadly disturbed by sin, and is at best always imperfect.

2*dly*. He is completely sanctified by his mystical union with Christ, his glorious head, and as a mema member of his body; in whom his old man is crucified and dead, and thus as part of Chrift, whatever Chrift is, he is.—The more the believer fees this, the more he longs for deliverance from all fin in himfelf, afhamed and humbled that he fhould be fo very unlike, not only to his head, but to what he himfelf is in his head.

No. XCI.

A POOR child of God may for a time (there is no faying how long) be holden down by the tyranny of fome accurfed befetting luft, whilft the inmoft language of his foul is, *O wretched man that I am, who fhall deliver me, &c.* (very different from thofe who offend of *malicious wickednefs.*) The ftreams of grace are all the while ftriving to clear the way, though running through a muddy, dirty channel; and at the very feafons, perhaps, when fin fhall have prevailed the moft fadly, and the poor creature fhall be faying, "Surely where there is fo much fin there can be no grace;" the Lord Jefus comes in with a tafte of pardoning love, and melts down the heart into filial contrition, faying as it were, " Ungrateful foul, I am ftill thy falvation; thy
" finfullnefs

" sinfullness can make no difference in my love;
" filthy and polluted as thou art in thyself, in me
" thou hast no sin at all; thy debts are all paid
" and cancelled, and nothing can be laid to thy
" charge. The sting of death was taken out by me,
" when I purchased thee with my own precious
" blood; and none (neither law, sin, death, hell,
" or the grave) have any demands upon thee,
" but what I have fully answered."

" O, replies the poor soul, but I must not yet
" venture to lay hold on Christ by faith, I must get
" the victory over my sin; I must repent and hum-
" ble myself; yea, and bring forth fruits meet
" for repentance, before I may conclude that I
" am interested in Christ, that God loves me,
" and that I am fit to die."

Such legal workings are sad enemies to peace, and tend to silence the voice of truth itself, yet they are what the most gracious souls are well acquainted with. Let us sift them a little, and we shall soon see that they strongly militate against the scripture method of salvation.

The grand mistake in these reasonings is, that they would thrust in something between sin and Christ, and find out some other remedy for a transgression of the law, besides the gospel.

It is a truth clear as the sun, that no soul shall be saved without repentance; but then the nature of repentance is grievously mistaken. Real repentance

repentance evidences a state of pardon and grace in a soul reconciled to God, and taken into covenant with him as an ungodly sinner; and thus being a state, and not consisting in any particular acts of humiliation (though such acts will always evidence such a state) it remains the same under all circumstances, as much as the grace and love of God which caused it, remain the same.

The first fruit of election, and union with Christ, is conviction of sin by the spirit; the second fruit, faith, by the same spirit; (though a degree of faith perhaps just sufficient to keep the soul from quite sinking, always accompanies conviction, in which sense they may be said to go together); the third, holiness, by the same spirit. All these worketh one and the same spirit; and they all, with every other privilege and blessing of the new covenant are included in the general expression of REPENTANCE UNTO LIFE.

Repentance, then, any more than its concomitant grace, faith, is not one day in the soul, and another day out of it; according as corruptions are more or less subdued, or according as sorrow for sin is more or less lively, but being a fruit of union with Christ, and of faith in him, as well as being of the very essence of conversion and regeneration, its habits remain ever the same.

H   in

in a child of God, however its actings may vary and be obscured; so that there is not a moment in which a believer is not a penitent, and *vice versâ* in which a penitent is not a believer: neither is there a moment in which the root and principle of sanctification is not alive in him, though the blossoms may seem to wither, or the fruit be blown off by some nipping wind of temptation.

Though these are most comfortable truths, which cannot be given up, without giving up the ground of gospel hope, yet are they far from giving encouragement to carnal security, or to a licentious walk. A true penitent, from the very nature of the grace that is in him, must feel himself a miserable creature under the prevalence of sin and corruption; his cry will be that of the Psalmist " *my misdeeds prevail against me.*" " O
" wretched man that I am! when I would do
" good, evil is present with me: I hate the sin
" which I commit, and I hate myself because of
" it. I approve of the law which would restrain
" me, and I consent unto its holiness, as well as to
" the just right it has over me, but alas the torrent
" of corruption bears down all my efforts and re-
" solutions, and I am led captive by the law of
" sin which is in my members."

In this condition the believer's assurance will be

be clouded. The fear of death will haunt him. He will be ready to conclude that he is deceiving his own soul: and that all his past experience was a delusion. He will pray and strive, and strive and pray for victory, and in God's due time he shall be sure to have it. He will plead scripture promises, and will search for scripture examples of saints in his own condition. Thus though the current of grace may appear to the poor soul itself to be clogged and stopped by the rubbish of corruption, and sin may have broken down all the dams of vows, resolutions and endeavours: yet all this while grace continues to flow, and that most freely too, by taking another channel, instructing the soul in deep self-knowledge and humility, and thereby defeating and over-ruling the malice of Satan in tempting him to sin.

XCII.

THE man who strives and fights against sin, though sin may often be suffered to overmatch him, is more assuredly a child of God, than he who never felt the plague of his own heart, or who thinks he has no sin to strive and fight against.

No. XCIII.

IT is a great proof of divine faith to believe God's affertions in fpight of inward darknefs; in fpight of ſtrong corruptions; in fpight of Satan's temptations; and in fpight of the world's lies.

No. XCIV.

WHAT reafon can be given, but that of God's fovereignty in election, why the moſt abandoned finners of mankind are often called to the knowledge of the gofpel, and made partakers of precious faith in the Son of God, whilſt multitudes of the decent and moral are left to perifh in their own deceivings, as dead to all fpiritual concerns as the very ſtones they tread upon?

Again, What other reafon can be given, why of two people in the fame pew, and hearing the fame fermon, the one fhall be favingly wrought upon, and the other perhaps go away contradicting and blafpheming?

3*dly.* For what other reafon were the apoſtles *forbidden of the Holy Ghoſt to preach the word*

in

in Afia; and when *they effayed to go to Bithynia*, were not fuffered by the Spirit to accomplish their purpose; whilst a vision appeared to Paul in the night, saying, *come over unto Macedonia and help us?* Were there not fouls in *Afia* and *Bithynia*, as well as in *Macedonia?* Undoubtedly there were. But the ministers of the gospel are sent forth to labor there, and there only, where the lord of the harvest has work for them to do in calling in his own people.

Oh! the depths both of the wisdom and mercy of God! How unfearchable are his ways, and his judgments past finding out!

No. XCV.

WERE I to receive some great guest into my house, particularly one from whose company I hoped to gain much happiness, much benefit, and much comfort, I should be careful to make my habitation as clean as possible, and to do nothing which might grieve, or offer insult to my welcome and profitable inmate.

But is this my conduct with regard to the blessed spirit of God? As a believer, *my body is the temple of the Holy Ghost which is in me.* Am I then careful not to defile that temple? not to insult and grieve the glorious inhabitant by sin, nor to quench the holy flame by a careless, negligent walk? Thou knowest, my soul, that the heavenly dove will take its flight from the mansions of impurity, and will not make its abode among the thorns of carking worldly cares. Oh! then walk humbly, warily, watchfully; keep thy conscience tender and void of offence; lest thou provoke the divine paraclete to withdraw himself, and lest thou lose the sensible presence of him whose favour is better than life.

No. XCVI.

IF we might form a judgment from the conduct of some high professors, we should be led to suppose that fasting, prayers, and alms-deeds of which such great things are spoken in scripture (not as meritorious, but as concomitants of the justified soul) are only fit trumpery for legalists and papists.

Again, If to visit the fatherless and widows in their affliction, and to keep ourselves unspotted from the world, be (as saith St. James) the distinguishing characteristic of pure and undefiled religion, we may well ask, where then is this genuine primitive Christianity to be found?

No. XCVII.

No. XCVII.

WHY does a believer so often find a weariness in God's service, and so much deadness and indisposition of heart in holy ordinances? The reason is, that man's nature and God's law are ever at variance. The fault is not in the law. God forbid. But through the weakness and sinfulness of the flesh, that becomes a burden, which is the believer's duty and privilege.

Still the believer's state in Christ is the same; and the obedience which he wants in himself is ever complete in his glorious head and surety. He will however pray and strive against this indisposedness of heart; and will be deeply humbled under his manifold short-comings; even whilst he takes Christ as his all and in all.

No. XCVIII.

HOW little is the sin of *selfishness* attended to, though it includes in it the breach of the whole second table at once.

No. XCIX.

No. XCIX.

THERE are but two sights which the Spirit shews to all the elect, as necessary to salvation; these are,

1*st*. The evil of sin.
2*dly*. The glory of Christ.

No. C.

THEY who place conviction of sin before pardon of sin, must thereby invert the order of the gospel, and place sanctification (in a measure) before justification. For it cannot be supposed that the Spirit dwells in my heart as a reprover or convincer of sin, and does not at the same time act as a sanctifier. Yet the common error teaches that I may be at the same moment convinced of sin, praying and striving against it, and yet unpardoned and under the law's curse.

But if conviction of sin is to precede the pardon of it, I should be glad to know how long the soul is to be under these convictions before it may expect pardon.

2*dly*.

2*dly.* What degree of conviction is necessary to prepare or qualify the soul for pardon.

3*dly.* If the convinced person should die before pardon, what would become of him in another world.

4*thly.* If conviction be previous to pardon, how comes it to pass that the apostles always address their new converts, as having received the atonement, as being reconciled when they were enemies, as those to whom God has already forgiven all trespasses. If not before, at least when they were first quickened ?. Ep. ii. 4. 5. 32. Col. i. 14. 21. Col. ii. 13. Col. iii. 13.

5*thly.* Is the convinced sinner at enmity with God? if he be not at enmity with him, he must be justified, since there is no middle state between wrath and pardon. If it be said that he is at enmity with God, then how can the spirit of grace be in him, and how can that spirit have shewn him the evil of sin, and how can he be longing after Christ and the blessings of salvation, which every convinced sinner most certainly does?

All these questions must necessarily arise, (and solve them who can) from that popular mistake, so baneful to the soul's comfort, and so clogging to the wheels of filial obedience, of placing conviction of sin or repentance before reconciliation, thereby making these to be something which we bring to

Christ,

Christ, instead of blessings we receive out of his fulness. And here I must observe, that this mistake itself arises from confounding pardon with the knowledge and sense of it, which it is the office of faith to draw from Christ, in whom the coming, weary, bruised sinner has already redemption and forgiveness, as much as the most advanced believer, though both at his first coming, as well as all his life afterwards, he stands in need of fresh application of atoning blood to the conscience; and fresh actings of repentance, on account of his continual transgressions of God's holy law, which the most exalted saint never keeps *perfectly* for a single moment.

No. CI.

FAITH and repentance can in no sound sense be called conditions of the new covenant; but they are those gifts and graces which the Lord works by his spirit in all those whom he has already taken into covenant with himself.

The very first motion of the soul towards God is the effect of his having loved, chosen and reconciled that soul unto himself in Christ Jesus. Even the day of the soul's espousals is when she is dead in trespasses and sins; and all her wedding ornaments are what she receives from her husband

husband after marriage; seeing she brings nothing to him but rags, yea, *filthy rags*, which cannot cover her nakedness.

All the soul's after-advancements in the divine life, are but steps whereby she rises up to the knowledge of those blessings which are treasured up for her in Christ, and which she receives out of his inexhaustible fullness. The first of these blessings, which the awakened, convinced soul is most particularly desirous of obtaining, is a sense of the forgiveness of sin. The life-giving Spirit having made the soul feel the burden of sin, she becomes weary and heavy laden; and through the weakness of her faith, not seeing her interest in Christ, she is ready to sink under the mighty load, and cannot be satisfied till the same Spirit proclaim and witness peace within her, and enable her to cry *Abba Father*, as the *earnest*, *seal* and *pledge* of her salvation. Various still are the soul's wants. She complains of her weakness, her ignorance, her deadness, her aversion to duty, her broken vows and resolutions, her strong corruptions, her manifold temptations, her sad desertions, worldly persecutions, &c. &c. Under all these, however, the Lord sustains her and brings her safe through every trial, till at last, in spight of all the efforts of sin, Satan and hell, he brings her where sorrow and sighing flee away; where the wicked cease from troubling, and where the weary are at rest.

No. CII.

No. CII.

THE moſt advanced faint knows not the thouſandth part of the depths of ſin that are in himſelf, nor the thouſandth part of the depths of that love that are in Chriſt.

No. CIII.

OUR not feeling ſin is no proof that we have it not. The non-ſenſation of ſin muſt be from ſpiritual death; the quick ſenſation thereof from ſpiritual life.

No. CIV.

THE ſelf-ſufficiency, ſelf-righteouſneſs and pride of the Phariſee, eſpecially of a Phariſee under a Chriſtian name, though he may be free from external offences, are more deteſtable in the eyes of God, and have more of the nature of Satan in them, (for that fiend cannot commit bodily ſins, ſuch as gluttony, drunkenneſs, uncleanneſs, &c.) than any outward abominations whatever.

No. CV.

No. CV.

THE man who goes about to humble himself and to amend after a fall into sin, before he looks to Christ, only gets hardness into his heart, and attempts to purge away sin by sin.

Nothing must stand between the sinner and the Savior. It is the believer's privilege and duty at all times to behold the Lamb of God, as having put away his sin; and thus looking to him the heart will be melted into sweet contrition.

Sin is the transgression of the law; and whosoever attempts to amend his life or to repent of his sins before he will claim his interest in Christ, not only perverts the design of the gospel, which holds forth Christ to sinners, merely as sinners, but tries to piece the law which he has broken, by giving it another rent; the law however curses the attempt to patch it up, as much as the first breach of it. If then you would have peace in your conscience, and holiness in your life, look to Jesus as having redeemed you from the curse of the law; and then you will obey the law from a principle of love and gratitude; yea, you will delight in it after the inner man; but it is impossible you can love that which is always lashing you, and which you fear in the end will damn you for your transgressions against it.

No. CVI.

No. CVI.

EITHER take Chrift or Mofes for your hufband; for you cannot have both. If you are married to Chrift, you are divorced from the law; (that is as a covenant by which you are to be faved, but not as a rule of life) : but if you are wedded to Mofes, you have no part in Chrift; and you will find Mofes to be as bloody an hufband as Zipporah did of old.

No. CVII.

A CHILD of God may perhaps be involved and entangled in fuch a manner, by fome particular temptation, as to be almoft at his wit's end. He may try to get away from it, but circumftances may be fo ordered that he cannot. He may ftrive and pray againft it, and yet may be permitted to be overcome by it. He may refolve and fall, and fall and refolve; and ftill may feem to be no nearer deliverance. Nay, he may feem for a feafon to have obtained deliverance; and yet Satan may foil him worfe than ever. (Oh! the diftrefs of a poor foul in

fuch

such depths.) He concludes himself cast out of God's remembrance. Cruel and rash professors, unacquainted with Satan's temptations, and ignorant of the power of sin in themselves, put him down as having no grace; but the Lord all the while sustains him, and seals instruction upon his heart; teaching him many humbling lessons, discovering to him his own weakness, shewing him where all his strength lies, and framing his spirit to bear with his brethren in like circumstances, and never to open the Pharisaic lip of pride and uncharitableness against them.

When these and any other useful ends, for which the temptation is suffered to remain, are answered, the Lord will mercifully remove it; and the soul shall know and taste more than ever it did before of the sweetness and extent of that gracious promise, *all things shall work together for good to those who love God, to those who are the called after his purpose.*

No. CVIII.

A STATE of spiritual life is not always to be known by a freedom from sin, nor by any external works of righteousness. Neither ought we to pronounce any man to be in a state of spiritual

tual death, becaufe he may have fallen into fin; feeing that this would be to condemn many of the moft eminent fcripture faints.

No. CIX.

GRACE and nature both act in a regenerate man; and both at once. Nature only acts in an unregenerate man. So that though fin be directly contrary to the Chriftian's walk, and as regenerate he hates it, and cannot commit it; yet the old nature in a believer can never love holinefs, but is at perpetual enmity with it, and can only be reconciled to fin. Hence that continual, never-ceafing war, in a child of God, between flefh and fpirit, fin and grace, the law in the members and the law in the mind.

No. CX.

THE man who is not watchful in his life and converfation, and who is not humble in his heart and deportment, as much defpifes Chrift in his kingly office, as the felf-righteous Pharifee defpifes him in his prieftly office; or as he that is wife in his own conceit, flights him in his prophetical office.

No. CXI.

No. CXI.

OF all the absurd cavils that ever were raised against the doctrines of grace, the most so is that of their being inimical to holiness and to good works.

Surely the boasted sons of reason must here have grievously deserted their own standard, and have fled for refuge to arguments which even a child might justly be ashamed of. Let us however give them their full force, and a patient hearing.

"If man (say they) be taken into covenant with God as a guilty helpless sinner, if (as some *enthusiasts* affirm) he hath redemption through the blood of Christ, even the forgiveness of his sins, according to the riches of God's grace, without any merit or works of his own previous to his acceptance, or as conditions thereof; the consequence must needs be, that having his heavy debt of sin freely remitted *without money and without price*, the sense of so much mercy and love will necessarily cause him to disobey the commands of his heavenly Father, who hath done such great things for him, and instead of abounding in good works, he will delight only in the practice of all manner of iniquity."

It may be said that I have dressed up the objection in a fool's coat in order to laugh at it. But in very deed it can wear no other, for turn the argument, and view it which way you will, it still comes round to this, viz. "The doctrine of "salvation by grace is unfriendly to morality and "to good works, it teaches men to live after their "own hearts lusts, and to wallow in ungodliness."

Thus cries many a grave, learned, dignified scribe, pleading for morality [which he perhaps cares little about] and being an advocate for good works [which 'tis more than probable he never practises.]

Let us now hear St. Paul's judgment of this matter; and let one text suffice, instead of a multitude which might be brought.

The grace of God which bringeth salvation, teacheth us that denying ungodliness and worldly lusts, we should live soberly, righteously, and godly in this present world. See now these two opinions in contrast.

Fashionable Divinity.	*St. Paul.*
The doctrine of salvation by grace is unfriendly to morality and to good works. It teaches men to live after their own hearts lusts, and to wallow in ungodliness.	The grace of God which bringeth salvation, teaches us that denying ungodliness and worldly lusts, we should live soberly, righteously and godly in this present world.

But

But behold, a greater than Paul is here! Our bleſſed Lord when he propounded the parable of the creditor and the two debtors (who were both *frankly forgiven*) to Simon the Phariſee, concluded the converſation with ſaying that *to whom much is forgiven, the ſame loveth much; but, to whom little is forgiven, the ſame loveth little.*

From ſcripture let us proceed to matter of fact both among clergy and laity.

Where is licentiouſneſs curbed? where is pure practical religion to be found? In the pulpits and congregations where works are inſiſted on as meritorious or conditional to juſtification? Or where we are told that *by grace we are ſaved through faith, and that not of ourſelves, it is the gift of God; not of works, leſt any man ſhould boaſt; for we are his workmanſhip created in Chriſt Jeſus unto good works, which God hath before ordained that we ſhould walk in them.*

Alas! Is it not evident that multitudes of moral ſermons produce nothing but multitudes of immoral actions! But where the glad tidings of ſalvation by grace, through faith alone in Chriſt Jeſus are founded, there the effects of that grace, and the fruits of that faith are to be ſeen in ſinners hearts being changed, and their lives and conver-

converfations being regulated according to God's holy word.

Let one ftriking example conclude our prefent meditation.

When that faithful minifter of Chrift, Mr. V———n, was vicar of H———d in Yorkfhire, he told me that a neighbouring clergyman, the Rev. Doctor L———, then vicar of H———x, one day addreffed him nearly in the following words: "Mr. V———n, I don't know how it is, but I "fhould really think that your doctrines of grace "and faith were calculated to make all your "hearers live in fin; and yet I muft own that "there is an aftonifhing reformation wrought in "your parifh; whereas I don't believe I ever "made one foul the better, though I have been "telling them their duty fo many years."

Mr. V———n fmiled at the Doctor's ingenuous confeffion, and frankly told him, "he would do well to burn all his old fermons, and try what preaching Chrift would do." But it is to be feared the advice was never followed.

I only add, that if all the *(merely)* moral fermons in the kingdom were to undergo the fame operation, though it would perhaps be the greateft, it would be one of the moft pleafing bonfires to God that ever was kindled.

No. CXII.

No. CXII.

THERE can be no rule of right and wrong but the will of God; this will is contained in the law of God, which is the written transcript of his mind, and is revealed to man in the ten commandments. Every believer in Christ acknowledges that he is dead to this law, and that this law is dead to him, as a covenant of works by which he is to hope for justification and salvation. But it is amazing that any believers should deny that the moral law remains in full force, as a rule of life to every one that is ingrafted into Christ by faith: and yet when they come to explain themselves, it shall be found, that this manner of speaking is by no means designed to cast dishonor on the law, or to set aside any of its commands.

Their language is, that being the freemen of Christ, they are no longer under the bondage of the law; and that the love of God is the grand principle and spring of all holy obedience.

It is agreed on all hands, that every believer is as much delivered from the law, as a covenant of works whereby he is to expect life, as a woman who is married a second time is freed from obedience to her firſt huſband, who is dead.

It is alſo agreed, that love is the grand motive of all holy obedience.

Wherein now is the difference? One Chriſtian ſays that the law is a believer's rule of life; another ſays the law is not a believer's rule of life. Yet both ſay that they are no longer under the law, as a covenant of works; and both ſay that the love of God is the Chriſtian's grand principle of obedience. Surely the diſpute is merely about words.

To affirm that *the law of love* is my rule, and not the moral law, is not leſs a diſtinction without a difference. For what is the moral law but the law of love? The ſum and ſubſtance of it is love. Love to God, and love to our neighbor. It may be objected, how can that be the law of love which ſhuts up every ſoul under wrath, and is itſelf a miniſtration of wrath, death, and condemnation? It may as reaſonably be aſked, how can God be *love*, and yet a *conſuming fire?* He is neverthelefs both. And as He is, ſo is his law. It levels all the curſes, thunderings and firings of Sinai, againſt every ſoul that is under it. But it is a law of love to the believer in Chriſt; his language (whether under the Old Teſtament or under the New) is, *O how I love thy law!*

I delight

delight in the law after the inward man. With *the mind, I serve the law of God,* pointing particularly to that law which faith, *Thou shalt not covet. This is the love of God, that we keep his commandments.*

Again, to make a distinction between *the royal law of love,* and the moral law, is to jump into the very error it tries to avoid; for it tends to the establishment of that Arminian whim, called *a remedial law of grace,* and causes the eternal immutable law of Jehovah, to stoop to the frailty of the creature.

Can any thing be plainer than the following texts to prove that the moral law and the law of love are one and the same?

Our Savior faith, *Thou shalt love the Lord thy God with all thy heart and mind, and soul and strength. This is the first and great commandment. And the second is like unto it,* viz. *Thou shalt love thy neighbor as thyself. On these two commandments hang all the law and the prophets.* Thus spake he who came to rescue the moral law from the false glosses which the Scribes and Pharisees had put upon it, and to enforce it in its extent, and spirituality, both for conviction of sin, and as a rule of life.

Let us hear now the language of his apostles. *Owe no man any thing, but to love one another;*

for

for he that loveth another, hath fulfilled the law. For this, thou shalt not commit adultery; thou shalt not kill; thou shalt not steal; thou shalt not bear false witness; thou shalt not covet: and if there be any other commandment, it is briefly comprehended in this saying, namely, *thou shalt love thy neighbor as thyself. Love worketh no ill to his neighbor; therefore love is the fulfilling of the law.* Rom. xiii. 8, 9, 10. Hear now another witness. *If ye fulfil the royal law, according to the scripture, Thou shalt love thy neighbour as thyself, ye do well. For he that said thou shalt not commit adultery, said also do not kill,* &c. &c. Jam. ii. 8, 9, 10, 11, 12.

Where now is the difference between the moral law and the law of love? and how can one be a believer's rule of life without the other, since in reality they are one and the same?

If it be said, that a believer takes the whole book of God to be his rule of life; and not the twentieth chapter of Exodus only;

I answer, that by taking the law to be my rule of life, I by no means reject, but on the contrary I adopt every other part of the sacred volume, (those shadows and ceremonies, which are passed away, excepted) as nothing is enjoined or forbidden therein which is not comprehended in the decalogue. Perfect love to God is the rule

of

of the firſt table. Love to our neighbor as to ourſelves, the rule of the ſecond table.

Let it now be conſidered, that this moral law, or *law of love*, or *law of liberty* to man in innocence, and to man redeemed, (being a law of wrath and terror only to man fallen) is that very ſame law which was written on Adam's heart in Paradiſe: the ſame which continued from Adam unto Moſes, when it was more diſtinctly promulgated from Mount Sinai: the ſame which accuſed or excuſed the conſciences of the Gentiles: the ſame which brings in the whole world guilty before its precepts: the ſame which our Lord in his firſt ſermon on the Mount, enforces and reſtores to its purity: the ſame which the apoſtles hold forth as the ſteady rule by which believers, under the influence of faith and love, are to walk.

Let theſe things be duly conſidered; and then let us briefly examine what miſchiefs will ariſe from rejecting the moral law as a believer's rule of life.

1ſt. By ſo doing, I ſet aſide the immutable eternal nature of the law, and *make void* the everlaſting obligation there is upon all reaſonable creatures to obey it.

2dly. Take away the law (as the ſtandard of good and evil, by which all actions are to be tried),

tried), and with it we take away sin also; *for where no law is, there is no transgression.*

3*dly.* Take away the law, as the test and criterion of right and wrong, and no believer on earth can tell when he offends God; for *I had not known sin,* (saith St. Paul) except the law had said *thou shalt not covet.*

4*thly.* Take away the law, as a believer's rule of life, and he ceases to see the continual need he stands in of Christ, to save him from his daily and hourly transgressions against it.

5*thly.* Take away the law, as that by which a believer is to square his conduct; and what other rule will you establish in its stead? Does faith in Christ teach us any other obedience than what is briefly comprehended in these words, *Thou shalt love the Lord thy God with all thy heart,* &c. *and thy neighbor as thyself.*

Now, Christian, let me ask thee, Is not the law thy rule of life? thou wilt answer, Yes, through grace I take the law as such; but alas! I fall sadly short in my obedience to it. Be humbled then for thy transgressions, and rejoice in this; *viz. that Christ is the end of the law for righteousness to every one that believeth; for what the law could not do, in that it was weak through the flesh, God sending his own Son in the likeness of sinful flesh, and for sin condemned sin in the flesh, that*

the

the righteoufnefs of the law might be fulfilled in us who walk not after the flefh, but after the fpirit.

Let us conclude this number by lamenting that any worthy laborious minifters fhould get themfelves branded with the name of Antinomians, and greatly hurt their own ufefulnefs, by denying the law to be a believer's rule of life, whilft in reality they are zealous for good works, and ftrenuous advocates for vital godlinefs, as well as crucified to the world, and exemplary in their own lives and converfations.

No. CXIII.

THOUGH the fins and backfliding of a believer cannot deftroy his intereft in Chrift, yet they may fo far deftroy his comfort (efpecially, if long perfifted in againft light and love, and of a foul nature), that even after he is delivered from the power of them, he may for a long time go bleeding under the wounds he has received from the commiffion of them.

The promife indeed is fure that God will not UTTERLY *take away his loving kindnefs* from one individual of the feed of grace, yet the threat is no lefs certain, that *he will vifit their iniquity with a rod, and their fin with fcourges*, not in a way of vindictive wrath, for that was all spent upon Chrift, but in a way of mercy and fatherly chaftifement. And, they only who know what it is to lofe the light of God's countenance after having enjoyed it for any time, can tell how fad and bitter a thing it is to be without the fenfible prefence of him whofe favor is better than life.

In fuch a ftate, however, it is a good fign when the foul is very earneft and importunate at the throne of grace to recover its former frames and feelings, and a very bad fign when fenfible confolations are looked upon as nothing worth.

The language of grace in thefe ftraits will be " O Lord, let me regain, yea more than regain my " firft love, and do my firft works. O let me " be zealous and repent; and remember from " whence I am fallen. O let thy love be again " fhed abroad in my poor difconfolate barren " heart by the Holy Ghoft. Do thou enable " me to cry *Abba Father*; and let thy fpirit bear " witnefs with my fpirit that I am a child of " God." If fuch be the cry of thy heart, thy prayer will be heard, and anfwered, only wait patiently the Lord's leifure.

No. CXIV.

No. CXIV.

HE was delivered for our offences, and raised again for our justification.

The justification here mentioned is certainly not of our persons before God; because this was effected by a work of Christ, previous to his resurrection, viz. by his obedience unto death; including his active and passive righteousness. But the justification in this place means a declarative acquittal before angels and men; in the same sense as good works justify our faith and profession: Jam. ii. 24. or as good words justify the soundness and integrity of the heart. *By thy words thou shalt be justified.* Mat. xii. 27. Or as *wisdom is justified of her children.* Luke, vii. 35. In this view of the text, it is animating, and full of consolation.

No. CXV.

AN healthy man may fall down and break a bone, (especially if he venture upon slippery places), which yet may be set again, and the limb be ſtronger than before, without impairing his conſtitution. But there is leſs hope of him who is in a ~~ſpiritual~~ _gradual_ decline, or in an atrophy.

As it is in temporals, ſo in ſpirituals: a ſtrong Chriſtian, by venturing too much on the ſlippery borders of temptation, may get a fearful tumble into the mire, and complain of broken bones as David did; but by grace he will riſe again, and walk more warily: whereas ſpiritual declenſions (at the root of which the canker worm of worldly-mindedneſs uſually lies concealed) eat up the very vitals of religion; and are the more dangerous as they advance more imperceptibly.

No. CXVI.

THE moſt advanced Chriſtians little ſuſpect how much ſelf-confidence and cleaving to the law of works ſtill remains in them. When they would ſoar heavenwards, and enjoy communion and fellowſhip with their Lord, they find that the wings of faith and love are clipped; they have no liberty in their conſciences, no acceſs with boldneſs to the throne of grace: *They feel not the love of God ſhed abroad in their hearts by the Holy Ghoſt*; obedience of courſe flags, duty is irkſome, and they cry *my leanneſs, my leanneſs*. Alas! my

soul,

soul, what dost thou lose by not living more by the faith of the Son of God? Examine thyself well, and thou wilt find that all thy dry barren frames and all thy unfruitfulness is owing to thy looking too much at self, and not enough to Christ. Pray then for an increase of the *precious faith of God's elect.* Lean less, rather not at all, on thyself, more on Christ. Then shalt thou soon find that *his strength shall be made perfect in thy weakness*; yea, that though *of thyself thou can'st do nothing*, yet that *thou can'st do all things through Christ who strengtheneth thee:* then shalt thou run with an enlarged heart the way of God's commandments; thy language shall be, Oh! how I love thy law: mortification, self-denial, and taking up the cross, though impossible to flesh and blood, shall even be delightful to thee: nay, thou shalt not only be *ready to suffer,* but, *if need be, to die for the Lord Jesus.*

Thus shall the sense of thy own weakness, sinfulness and nothingness bring glory to God and profit to thyself.

No. CXVII.

No. CXVII.

THERE are those who think they ought never to pray but when they find their hearts drawn out by the spirit of grace and supplication, inviting them as it were to that holy exercise.

This notion appears to have no foundation in scripture; yea, it seems directly contrary to scripture, and if given way to, may in the end leave the soul totally prayerless, if not gracelefs.

I would rather follow the example of Luther, who always hastened to the throne of grace, when he found the greatest indisposition to go thither; and by that means often warmed a cold heart at the fire of God's altar.

Under the law if the sacrifice would not go willingly, it was to be dragged. And under the gospel, *the kingdom of heaven suffereth violence, and the violent take it by force.*

No. CXVIII.

I HAVE often been astonished that any good men should be against making a general tender of the gospel to sinners.

It will be said, that none have interest in gospel blessings but believers. Granted. But still their right and title to the gospel is not founded on their being believers; but merely on their being sinners, destitute of every spark of faith, grace, or goodness.

But if the gospel is to be preached only to believers, or to a gathered church, to whom did the apostles preach it before any souls were converted to the faith? certainly not to believers, none of which were perhaps before them in the multitudes they addressed, but *to sinners* as such, who by believing the gospel report became interested in the salvation it holds forth.

It is trifling to say that a general offer supposes a power in the sinner to believe and to accept that offer. This is by no means the case; but it supposes that God accompanies his own word with his own power. And that he directs that arrow to the hearts of his own people, which the preacher shoots by *drawing the bow at a venture*. The almighty *fiat* originally spake the world out of nothing: and surely he who gives the command to believe and to arise from the dead, can clothe that mandate with a quickening efficacy, so that elect souls shall come out of the grave of unbelief and live.——" Thus (saith Bp. Beveridge)
" we find in Israel's return from Babylon to
" Jerusalem; though Cyrus made proclama-
" tion

"tion that whoever would might go up to wor-
"ſhip at the holy city, Ezra i. 3. yet there were
"none that accepted the offer *but thoſe whoſe
ſpirit God had raiſed to go up. v. 5.* So here,
"though God doth as it were proclaim to all the
"world, that whoſoever will come to Chriſt ſhall
"certainly be ſaved, yet it is certain none can will
"to come unleſs God enable them."

Bp. Beveridge's Private Thoughts.

Under the law, the prophets made the general offer to ſinners: Ezekiel particularly addreſſed himſelf to the dry bones, *O ye dry bones, hear ye the word of the Lord.* And under the goſpel, our Lord and his apoſtles frequently called to the dead in ſin, *to repent and to believe the goſpel*: nay St. Peter actually excites *Simon Magus*, (though then *in the gall of bitterneſs and bond of iniquity*) both to repentance and to prayer.—In a word, they made the general tender to ſinners, *whoſoever will let him come and take of the water of life freely*, though only *as many as were ordained to eternal life believed.*

It was the departing command of our bleſſed Lord to his diſciples. *Preach the goſpel to every creature.* In which command, certainly, no one creature is excepted. Much leſs millions and millions of creatures, which would be the caſe, if the offer of Chriſt were to be made only to believers, who

are

are already interested in him. So that the command seems worded in such a manner as expressly to take in the unconverted.

Besides, how could any be left without excuse at the great day for rejecting the gospel offer, if that offer never were made to them?

Lastly. It is a notorious fact that God blesses and owns that preaching in which there are solemn adresses to sinners ; whereas those who only apply themselves to believers are seldom made instrumental in adding to their number.

Much has been said against a pious minister for telling his congregation that " he charged them all to meet him at God's right hand at the great day." The expression is a strong one, yet surely all he meant was this. " If you perish,
" your blood be on your own heads, I have now
" solemnly warned you. I have delivered my
" own message, and my own soul. If you
" neglect this warning, you will die eternally.
" If you turn to God in consequence of it, I
" shall meet you as my joy and crown of re-
" joicing at the right hand of God before an as-
" sembled world."

In this sense, and certainly no other was intended, the expression was not only allowable, but sound, and no objection can reasonably lie

against

againſt it, but what will equally lie againſt the prophet Ezekiel for his expoſtulations with the rebellious houſe of Iſrael, *to turn* THEMSELVES *and live.*

No. CXIX.

THE believer carries no worſe enemy about him than *ſpiritual ſloth*. This foe is ſo much the more ſubtle as it does not make its attacks ſuddenly, but creeps upon him unawares; and the more dangerous, as it aſſaults both ſoul and body; and both ſoul and body are too ready to ſide with it againſt themſelves. Other ſins are for the moſt part either fleſhly or ſpiritual. Among the former, are gluttony, drunkenneſs, uncleanneſs, &c. Among the latter, pride, envy, malice, hatred, &c. but *ſpiritual ſloth* affects both body and mind, and whoſoever gives way to it deprives himſelf of many bleſſings which are promiſed to ſtriving, diligent, circumſpect ſouls.

It may be ſaid that God in the everlaſting covenant has ſet down and decreed what degrees of grace, knowledge, and fruitfulneſs all his people ſhould arrive at; and therefore all their ſtriving

striving and praying will not add a tittle thereto, or diminish an atom therefrom.

I answer, that though this be a scriptural truth, and when rightly taken by a poor seeking soul complaining of barrenness, a very comfortable one, yet the language of the objection is totally unscriptural, and argues only for the abuse, not for the use of the doctrine; and whosoever can rest satisfied under the notion that he has as much grace and fruitfulness as God before ordained that he should have, has reason to suspect that he may be in the number of those whom God has before ordained to condemnation; since a regenerate heart cannot exist without its distinguishing characteristic, an *hungring and thirsting after righteousness.*

Most certain it is, that known unto God are all his works; and that every the most minute circumstance which concerns his church, and every individual member thereof, is exactly and wisely ordered; insomuch that as nothing comes by chance, so nothing can be altered to be otherwise than it is.

But it is equally certain, that secret things belong unto God, whose decrees are all accomplished in the use of appointed means; and that a man may as reasonably expect to become sober by drinking drams, or to get fat by starving himself to death, as any soul may suppose he can be admitted into heaven without *striving* to enter in at the strait gate.

Those whom the Lord in his counsel *(secret to us)* hath predestinated unto eternal life, he hath also *predestinated to be conformed to the image of his own dear Son*, in their way thither; and such as are branches ingrafted into Christ the true vine, are *purged by the heavenly husbandman that they should bring forth much fruit.*

Again, though all gospel blessings are treasured up in Christ, yet they are promised to *knocking, seeking, asking* souls, and whosoever calls himself a believer, and has not found in the course of his experience, that the way to thrive in his soul, is to live near to God, fighting against sin in the strength of Christ, and in a diligent use of the means of grace, may well call in question the truth of his faith, and doubt whether *the root of the matter*, as Job speaks, was ever really in him.

But it is in vain to waste words. All the exhortations, commands and threats, with which the scripture abounds, are levelled against this complicated evil, *spiritual sloth*. O then, my soul, take unto thee the whole armour of God; and above all, the shield of faith. Up, up, and be doing. Strive earnestly; fight manfully; redeem

the

the time. Death, judgment, eternity are at hand: and who knows what a day may bring forth? Whatever be out of thy fight, as to the Lord's decrees, his revealed will is before thy eyes; and *this is the will of God, even your sanctification.*

Inftead therefore of perplexing thyfelf with vain reafonings, as to the purpofes of God concerning thy fpiritual growth and attainments, behold both *his* defigns and *thy* duty reconciled, and pointed out by the apoftle. *Work out your own falvation with fear and trembling; for it is God that worketh in you of his good pleafure.*

No. CXX.

THOUGH the temptations of God's people are various, according to the refpective circumftances and temperament of the parties, yet there are very few, perhaps no real Chriftians, who have not been diftreffed on the three following accounts.

1*ft*. Great wanderings and great deadnefs in prayer.

2*dly*. Blafphemous and other horrible thoughts, particularly at the very feafons when they would moft wifh to be freed from thofe thoughts.

3*dly*.

3*dly.* Doubts about the truth of the scriptures, extending to question even the very being of a God.

These are matters that the vassals of Satan seldom perplex themselves about. But if that fiend of darkness cannot keep one of Christ's sheep out of heaven, he will make them go limping thither if he can.

No. CXXI.

IT is absolutely impossible that the world should have any idea either of the joys or sorrows of God's people; because both the one and the other are peculiar to grace; and are such as nature is totally incapable of taking any part in.

No. CXXII.

EVERY believer, who has attained a right knowledge of himself, will acknowledge with blessed Bradford the martyr, then Dean of St. Paul's, that the seeds of every sin that ever was or can be committed, are in his own heart and nature.

This

This knowledge affords the Christian great cause of humility. But it affords him greater still, that the Lord hath loved him in this state of filth, rebellion and apostacy; yea hath washed him so pure in the blood of his son, that the moral law itself can find no speck of sin upon him. And that, by the power of the Holy Ghost, he chooses God for his portion, and turns his back on the world, the flesh, and the devil.

No. CXXIII.

WHAT rich food for a believing soul is there in this one promise, *" Call upon me in the day of trouble, and I will deliver thee?"* Blessed be thy name, O Lord, for the full experience that one poor sinner has repeatedly had of the power and efficacy of this promise, even when heart and flesh were ready to fail; and when his own sin and baseness had been the cause of his distress; so that he could truly adopt the prophet's exclamation: *O Israel, thou hast destroyed thyself; but in me is thy help.*

No. CXXIV.

THE man who does not see that the world is his enemy, who does not feel his danger from its snares and entanglements, and, even from its allowable comforts; and who does not watch and pray against a worldly mind, is of all others the fastest bound with the world's chains.

Lord, evermore give me that faith which overcometh the world; that so I may be crucified unto the world, and the world unto me.

No. CXXV.

IT were much to be wished, that the ministers of the gospel would not only lift up their voices against the outward abominations of drunkenness, profaneness, sabbath-breaking, uncleanness, &c. but that they wou'd more frequently shew their hearers the diabolical nature of spiritual wickedness; such as pride, envy, malice, hatred, revenge, covetousness, self-will, uncharitableness; with many others which spring

from

from the fame infernal root, and under the power of which multitudes live and die, without ever being made fenfible of their accurfed quality and heinous gilt.

But oh! how fad is it to fee profeffors of the religion of the meek and lovely Jefus, under the influence and dominion of thefe Satanical tempers, even whilft *the outfide of the platter* is made exceedingly white and clean, and there whilft is an exact *talkative* knowledge of gofpel doctrines; with a running about to hear different preachers, perhaps three or four times a week; an hymn book, a ticket, and a little Bible, being the ufual pocket furniture. Often alas! have I been witnefs to thefe things. Yet fure I am that it was the conftant practice of our Lord and of his apoftles to bear the fame teftimony againft thefe truly devilifh difpofitions, as againft adultery, fornication, drunkennefs, theft and murder. *Out of the heart* (faith Chrift) *proceed evil thoughts, adulteries, fornications, murders, thefts, covetoufnefs, deceit, lafcivioufnefs, an evil eye, blafphemy, pride, foolifhnefs.* Mark, vii. 21, 22. So the apoftle Paul, enumerating the works of the flefh, claffes *hatred, variance, emulations, wrath, ftrife, envyings,* with *adulteries, murders, drunkennefs, revellings, and fuch like.* Gal. v. 21. And in v. 26. he adds, *let us not be defirous of vain glory,*

glory, provoking one another, envying one another. The Church of England too teaches all her members to pray againſt *pride, vain glory and hypocriſy, envy, hatred and malice,* with the ſame breath that they ſupplicate deliverance from fornication, and all other deadly ſin. And in the exhortation before the communion, ſhe not only ranks malice and envy with blaſphemy and adultery, but warns all perſons who are under the power of theſe ſins, not to approach the Lord's table. However deteſtable in God's pure eyes, corporeal ſins, ſuch as gluttony, drunkenneſs, uncleanneſs, &c. may be, yet ſpiritual iniquities are more of the eſſence of the fallen nature, as well of the nature of Satan himſelf than thoſe are: but both the one and other ſpring from the ſame poiſoned fountain, viz. the original corruption and apoſtacy of man, and therefore they are both equally denominated by *the works of the fleſh*; nay, they are both alike called *filthineſs,* the ſpirit as well as the fleſh having its own groſs pollutions; and the ſame remedy is pointed out in ſcripture for the cure of one as the other, viz. faith in the word of promiſe. *Having therefore, dearly beloved, theſe promiſes, let us cleanſe ourſelves from all* FILTHINESS *of the fleſh and ſpirit, perfecting holineſs in the fear of God.* 2 Cor. vii. 1. *wherefore* (ſaith another apoſtle) *laying aſide all*

malice

malice and all guile, and hypocrisies, and envyings, &c. as new born babes desire the sincere milk of the word. 1 Pet. xxi. 2. Now, in all this black catalogue there is not a sin named but what the spiritual, or I should rather say, the immaterial part of man commits, and not one that his material part, the body, can have any share in; and yet the exhortation against them is not at all less strong than against the outward abominations specified in the eleventh verse of that same chapter. *Dearly beloved, I beseech you as strangers and pilgrims, abstain from fleshly lusts, which war against the soul.* St. Paul again mentions these spiritual filthinesses as what highly grieve the Holy Spirit of God. *Grieve not the Holy Spirit whereby ye are sealed unto the day of redemption. Let all bitterness, and wrath, and anger, and clamour and evil-speaking be put away from you, with all* MALICE.

Examine thyself then, my soul, how it stands with thee in this matter; since I may be a flourishing professor outwardly, and yet no better than a painted sepulchre inwardly. Am I humbled for my spiritual filthiness? Do I mourn over the heart-risings of pride, envy, malice, hatred, hypocrisy, unbelief, revenge, with the whole train of evil thoughts, which come from within and defile the man? Have I put on the Lord Jesus

Jesus Christ? And have I, though but in a small degree, the mind that was in him? Am I clothed with humility, and am I bringing forth the fruits of the spirit, being kind, tender-hearted, forgiving others, even as God for Christ's sake *hath* forgiven me? If this be my case, the humbling sense I have of the spiritual evils with which my nature abounds, is a full proof that they have not the dominion over me; but that I am in the happy number of those whose self-knowledge keeps them low in their own eyes, and causeth them to take Christ as their *all in all.*

No. CXXVI.

WHATEVER be left undone, my soul, these things must be thy daily employment; and unless thou art in a bad state of spiritual health, they will be so.

To be much in prayer and meditation.

Never to miss reading some portion of God's *pure* word.

To ransack every corner of a *deceitful and desperately wicked heart.*

To keep a watch over every rising thought, as well as over every word and action.

To

To be particularly on thy guard against any *besetting* evil.

To bring the *solemn, solemn, solemn* hour of departure often before thy eyes.

In whatever business thy hands are engaged, this must be thy daily work, and that of every one who would be found watching, and who has taken Christ as his prophet, priest, and king.

No. CXXVII.

THERE is perhaps no part of a minister's office more arduous than to know how to encourage weak faith, and at the same time to discourage unbelief: and yet the difficulty seems to lie in distinguishing between that unbelief, which dishonors God, by rejecting, or rather by doubting the testimony of his word; and, that which makes the soul question its own particular interest in the promises. Of the former kind was that of the disciples, when our Lord *upbraided them with their unbelief and hardness of heart, because they believed not them which had seen him after he was risen.* Mark, xvi. 14. Luke, xxiv. 25. Of the latter kind was that of poor Peter, who, when he was ready to sink, cried out *Lord save, I perish.* Whilst Jesus very gently, if at all, rebuked

buked his fears and misgivings, he cherished and comforted his weak faith. *O thou of little faith, wherefore didst thou doubt?* Of the same kind is that of every humble convinced sinner, weary with doubts, and heavy laden with fears; and whosoever tells a poor, penitent, awakened soul, that his doubts and fears increase his guilt, which must be the case if they are sinful, rubs salt into the wounds, when he should apply oil; and acts but too like the unfaithful shepherds of old, against whom the Lord thus complains by the mouth of his prophet. *The diseased have ye not strengthened, neither have ye healed that which was sick, neither have ye bound up that which was broken.* Ezek. xxxiv. 4.

A poor doubting soul ought not (indeed he cannot) rest satisfied in such a state, but ought to be continually looking to Jesus to increase his faith. *Compare this* No. *with* No. LVIII. p. 46.

No. CXXVIII.

IF those who are apt to take things amiss in others, would carefully examine their own hearts, they would generally find this temper owing to something *very much amiss* in themselves.

felves. Pride and felf-will are commonly the parents of it.

No. CXXIX.

THERE are some persons who, so long as they fancy that you look upon them to be all perfection, will be exceedingly pleased with you; but if they have let out their corruptions before you, and they think you see them in their true colours, they immediately dislike you.

When this temper appears, it proves to a certainty, that all their seeming love to you, was only love to themselves; and that as the pride of being thought something first begat it, so when they are conscious that you can no longer have the same opinion of them which you had at first, pride meeting with a mortification, they can no longer *bear you*, merely because you *know them*. For the very same reason it is, that others always dislike those whom they themselves have behaved ill to.

But perhaps the most dreadful of all spiritual filthiness is that of one minister of Christ envying another minister's gifts and usefulness, even to a degree of malice which cannot bear to hear them commended.

That the human heart is capable of this, is too certain: But surely those who feel any thing of the fort rising in their bosoms, should immediately retire, and pray for that person, or minister, whom they find to be the object of this Satanical temper.

And as the whole train of spiritual evils *proceed from within*, what need have all to be earnest at the throne of grace that they may obtain that *precious faith*, by which alone the heart can be purified, and be made a fit temple for the sweet spirit of love to dwell in.

No. CXXX.

THE Lord passes his love over upon a soul, and takes it into covenant with himself, whilst it is in a state of enmity and rebellion against him, and dead in trespasses and sins. But the soul cannot be taken into covenant with God, and yet remain unpardoned; for if the covenant be not a covenant of peace and reconciliation, and if it do not actually re-instate the soul into that favor with God, which was forfeited by the fall, it does nothing.

Every elect sinner, then, is a partaker of the gospel salvation, and is brought into a state of reconciliation, whilst he is *in his blood*, totally unconverted, *an enemy to God, ungodly, without strength*, without faith, without repentance, or any one holy disposition. Rom. v. 6, 7, 8, 9, 10.

In consequence of the Lord's having loved, betrothed and espoused to himself the elect sinner in all his enmity and in all his filthiness, and having freely forgiven him all trespasses, the quickening spirit visits his heart in a way of conviction of sin, Col. i. 21, 22. Col. ii. 13, 14. Eph. ii. 4, 5. discovering to him its *exceeding sinfulness*, filling him with a restless desire to be delivered from its guilt, punishment and power; and causing him anxiously to seek out for that remedy which the scripture holds forth.

Now will any one affirm, that the soul in such a state, is under the curse of the law; that it is not taken into covenant with God; and that it hath no union with Christ?

What! whilst the spirit of Christ has possession of the heart! Surely such an assertion is big with absurdity, and at once says, that there is and is not reconciliation; and that though Christ be in the sinner, and one with him, yet that the sinner is not in Christ, and not one with him.

It will be said, that conviction of sin precedes faith and regeneration, and that a sinner cannot be interested in any of the gospel blessings till he believes, nor till he is regenerate and born again:

I answer, Faith doth indeed discover to the elect sinner, that he is taken into covenant with God; doth shew him that the law's curse is removed from him to his surety; and that through faith it is that the Spirit manifests to the soul its adoption into the family of God; yea, that it is through faith only, the elect sinner receives Christ in all his offices, as his prophet, priest, and king; and therefore it is, that such great things are spoken of faith, and that it is said to justify: yet, who but an ideot in divinity, would say that the grace of faith justifies, or that it reconciles to God, any otherwise than by laying hold of, or making known to the elect soul that perfect righteousness which it hath in Christ, its head; of whom the soul is *apprehended* before it *apprehends* Christ.

In a word, to say that there is no being in covenant with God, no interest in gospel blessings, no pardon, reconciliation, or justification, no union with Christ, no redemption from the curse of the law, no acceptance with God (for these are synonimous terms) before conviction of sin, nor before faith and regeneration, is to

make

make all that dependent upon inherent grace, which is itself the ground and foundation of that very grace; consequently it makes the cause to flow from the effect, instead of the effect from the cause; at the same time that it favors too much of a refined sort of justification by works, and holds forth a very uncomfortable idea to distressed, awakened consciences.

It will not however be found so certain as some imagine, that conviction of sin precedes faith and regeneration. The truth is, that in order of time they all take place together, insomuch that no one can be convinced of sin without a degree of faith in the scripture testimony; and no one is either convinced of sin, or has faith without being born again; a convinced, unregenerate believer being a contradiction in terms. What therefore God hath joined together, let no man put asunder.

But though conviction of sin, faith and regeneration all take place at once, and are all complete works of God, as much as justification itself is complete (since no one can be half a convinced sinner, half a believer, half born again, any more than he can be half justified) yet do they all admit of degrees and growth, though justification admits of neither. That is to say, the soul that is convinced of sin, grows in the knowledge of the evil, and of the *exceeding sinfulness of sin*; and still attains greater degrees of this knowledge as it advances in the divine life, though it's original conviction be a perfect work of the spirit.

2*dly*. The soul that upon it's first awakening has but faith enough to put it on the flight to Christ, yea though his faith be but as a grain of mustard-seed, and though it be impeded in it's progress by mountains of self-righteousness, and by dark thick clouds of unbelief, has as much received a complete Savior as the most advanced believer, though it may be many years before such a soul attains to the full assurance of faith, and perhaps may never attain to it at all.

3*dly*. The soul which is thus far convinced of sin, and is thus far looking to Christ, is as much born again of the spirit, and new created, as the most exalted saint can be, but as the natural babe grows in all its parts, so doth the new born spiritual babe grow in grace, and in the knowledge of our Lord and Savior Jesus Christ. In this sense though regeneration itself be at first perfect, yet doth the new born child of grace grow and increase till it arrive at the full stature of a young man and father in Christ.

In brief there can be no intermediate state, or moment between spiritual death and spiritual life; between unbelief and faith; between unregeneracy and being born again; and therefore the soul that

has

has experienced the firſt quickening influences or the Holy Ghoſt, is as much paſſed from death unto life, and as much freed from curſe and condemnation as if he were already in Heaven: And all the works and duties of ſuch an one are acceptable to God in Chriſt, though done under much ſlaviſh fear and bondage of ſpirit, till the Holy Ghoſt cries abba father in the heart, and manifeſts to the ſoul it's adoption and intereſt in all the goſpel promiſes and new covenant bleſſings, filling it with joy and peace in believing, and giving it that perfect love which caſteth out all tormenting fear. Yet even after this, the ſoul may again have it's dark trembling fits, and loſe the ſenſe of Chriſt's love, though it never loſes the love of Chriſt himſelf.

No. CXXXI.

THE firſt ſpark of light, and the firſt motion of ſpiritual life in the heart of a ſinner, muſt come from him who is the light and the life of men. But Chriſt cannot dwell in the heart, unleſs there be union with him, and whoſoever is thus paſſed from death unto life is not under condemnation.

Again. An unbeliever cannot put forth any act of ſpiritual life, ſeeing he himſelf is dead in

ſin:

sin: and every such act which a believer puts forth is the act of a justified person.

These are self-evident truths to an enlightened mind; and the necessary conclusions resulting from them must be.

1st. That union and justification precede conviction of sin; though the knowledge of these blessings be subsequent thereto.

2dly. That justification is passed over to the soul, whilst it is spiritually dead.

3dly. That repentance does not fit or prepare any soul for pardoning mercy, but is a proof that the soul has received mercy as an ungodly sinner.

4thly. That to preach up humiliation and reformation, in order to qualify the soul for pardon, is in effect to preach the law instead of the gospel.

5thly. That all such preachers require living works from dead men, and the obedience of God's children from such as are children of wrath.

6thly. That both faith and repentance are fruits of union with Christ, and of reconciliation through his blood.

7thly. That the life of a believer is *hid with Christ in God.*

8thly. That *because Christ liveth, he shall live also.*

9thly. That where the Holy Spirit dwells in

the heart by faith, there the fruits of that Spirit muſt appear in the life.

10*thly.* That where Chriſt, the living head of his church, now is, there every living member muſt alſo be.

The above concluſions will pave the way for the following abſurdities, which are neceſſarily involved in the common popular miſtake of placing conviction of ſin by the ſpirit of Chriſt, before pardon of ſin by the merit of Chriſt.

To ſay, that a man has the grace of God in his heart, and that he is made a partaker of the life-giving ſpirit, convincing him of the evil of ſin, and making him willing to receive Chriſt in all his offices, and yet that his perſon is under condemnation, is full of groſs contradictions. It is to make a man at once dead, and alive; a child of light, and a child of darkneſs; a believer, and an unbeliever; regenerate, and carnal; one with Chriſt, and yet at enmity with him.

Into all theſe, and a thouſand more abſurdities, as deſtructive of the ſoul's peace as ſubverſive of pure goſpel truth, do they fall into, who inſtead of freely holding up Chriſt to ſinners as ſuch, tell poor ſouls that *by grace* they muſt repent, *by grace* they muſt amend their lives, *by grace* they muſt do this, that and the other, and then there is no doubt but God will pardon them, and give them an intereſt in Chriſt; yet this is the language of

many

many ministers—yea, of many who I am persuaded not only mean well, but who are really the children of God, and who wish to bring souls to Christ, and whose labors the Lord blesses, notwithstanding the remaining darkness by which, in a pious sincerity and an honest fear and jealousy for the interests of holiness, they keep many of the Lord's people in continual bondage and distress of conscience, laboring as it were in the fires, and calling for *the whole tale of bricks*, without *giving straw* to make one: For though they should tell sinners of grace in Christ from morning till night, that grace is no grace to me, any more than it is to a devil or to a damned spirit, unless I receive it out of the fullness of Christ, which I can no otherwise do, but as I have first received Christ himself, and am one with him. The graft must be put into the tree before it can derive sap and nourishment from that tree; so the believer must be united to Christ, the head of influence, before he can receive grace from him, as a branch engrafted into the true vine; and it is impossible he should be so united and engrafted, and still remain a child of wrath, in a state of enmity against God; and if not in a state of enmity, then he must be in a state of reconciliation: unless we affirm with the papists, that justification is progressive, and dependent on the conduct of the creature.

These

These truths are so demonstrable and self-evident, that it is amazing how so many good and gracious souls can stumble at them: But as this view of things entirely takes the whole business of salvation out of the sinner's hands, and places it in the Savior's, no wonder we are so unwilling to submit to it.

I am, however, aware of an objection which may be raised against the doctrine.

It may be asked, how can there be union between Christ and the soul, before the bond of that union be cemented by the Spirit given from Christ, working faith in the sinner's heart?

I answer, that the union and oneness which subsists before faith, is through Christ the fœderal head and representative of his church, having actually taken the flesh and blood of all the elect seed, who were chosen with him and in him as members and very parts of his body; yea, as *bone of his bone*, and *flesh of his flesh*; and to whom grace was given in him before the foundation of the world: but the manifestation of this union, and the sinner's own knowledge of it, is by the faith of the operation of God, at the time of effectual calling.

Whilst these truths open a more glorious display of divine grace and love, they bring with them at the same time the fullest confirmation of the

the doctrines of unconditional election, and of the final perseverance of every soul that was given to Christ in the covenant of redemption: and in this view of them they were embraced by *Theodore Beza*, and the most eminent men among the Reformers. And though they were on this account termed *Supralapsarians*, yet it will perhaps be difficult to split the hair between them and others of the Reformers who, for distinction sake, were called *Sublapsarians*.

No. CXXXII.

A BELIEVER is *the light of the world. The salt of the earth. A city set on an hill. A child of God. A friend of God. An heir of God. A joint-heir with Christ.* He is a partaker of the divine nature. He is one with Christ, and Christ is one with him. He is espoused and married unto Christ. He is a member of Christ's body. He is bone of Christ's bone, and flesh of Christ's flesh. Christ liveth in him; dwells in his heart; sups with him, and he sups with Christ. The Father, Son, and Spirit (the blessed Trinity in unity) *make their abode with him*, and condescend to have *fellowship and communion with him*. He

hath

hath put on Christ; is in Christ; is crucified with Christ; is risen with Christ; is set down in heavenly places with Christ.

Oh! love, passing knowledge. What manner of persons ought we to be, in all holy conversation and godliness?

No. CXXXIII.

It is a rash assertion (though not unfrequently heard) that any man will be condemned on account of his own righteousness and good works; since no one will be punished but for his unrighteousness and for his bad works. Were his own righteousness and works really such as could bear the test of God's law, instead of being condemned for them, he would be justified by them; but as they fall infinitely short of what that pure, just, and holy law demands, they become sins and misdeeds, instead of good and righteous works: and therefore it is that the truth and justice of God cannot but inflict the deserved penalty upon them, according to his own declaration. Cursed is every one that continueth not in all things which are written in the book of the law to do them. The law then is a ministration of death and condemnation even to those who observe it the most exactly. The gospel is a ministration of righteousness (of the justifying righteousness of Christ) to all that truly believe.

And here it is worthy of observation, that though we render the words, καλα εργα, GOOD WORKS, yet the exact translation is *ornamental works, i. e.* such works whereby we adorn the doctrine of God our Savior.

No. CXXXIV.

THOUGH the word imputation is made use of in scripture, as best suited to our capacities, and as expressive of the vicarious underdertakings of the Lord Christ: Yet is the righteousness of Christ more than imputed to a believer. It was as much wrought out by all the spiritual seed, in their second living fœderal head, as the law was broken by all the natural seed, in their first fœderal head, Adam; in whom, as saith the apostle, all have sinned.

In the same manner, then, as by the disobedience of one, many were made sinners; by the obedience of one, shall many be made righteous. And if all the elect really wrought out a perfect righteousness in Christ, as being one with him; then they must have union with him, and this righteousness must

muſt be theirs, even before it is *revealed to them* (as the ſame apoſtle ſpeaks) *by faith :* though, as conſidered in the firſt Adam, they are by nature children of wrath, even as others.

No. CXXXV.

THERE are few things which prove the diſorder which is introduced into the world by the fall, more than the ſeverity with which dumb creatures are too often uſed by thoſe to whom God hath placed them under ſubjection.

It is certain that there are many unconverted perſons (eſpecially among the amiable ſex) who from a certain contexture of conſtitution, feel much for animals in diſtreſs, and who love to make them happy; ſurely then all thoſe, whoſe feelings are heightened by religion, and who know that all animals, in their degree, partake of the miſeries of the general apoſtacy, and that *the whole creation travaileth and groaneth* on this account, ought to do all in their power to bring things back to their original ſtate in Paradiſe, where I doubt not but every creature flocked about the happy pair in innocence, and placed the fulleſt confidence in their primæval lord. And were man now to ſhew him-

himself kind and tender-hearted towards them, it is certain that confidence would in a great measure be recovered, as has been proved in various instances (particularly in the amity subsisting between the excellent Mr. Cowper, author of the Poems, and his hare); and the kingdoms of this world, in respect of the intercourse and happiness among the different orders of beings, become a peaceful millenium state. The wisest man that ever lived, (he who is emphatically the wisdom of God excepted) has left it on record, that *the merciful man is merciful to his beast*; by which it is evident, that it is as much the character of one who fears God, to be indulgent to the brute creation, as it is for him to pray or to give alms.

―――The meanest things that are,
As free to live, and to enjoy that life,
As God was free to form them at the first,
Who in his sovereign mercy made them all.
Ye therefore who love mercy, teach your sons
To love it too.
Cowper.

No. CXXXVI.

No. CXXXVI.

THERE can perhaps be no better judgment formed of a man's state Godward, than by the estimate he has of the world. Every real Christian looks upon the world as his soul's foe, and whilst he is *in* the world, is not *of* the world: nay even when the world puts on the most alluring face, he accounts its smiles as those of a deceitful harlot, and the language of his heart is, *Thou art my portion, O Lord. Whom have I in heaven but thee, and there is none upon earth that I desire in comparison of thee?* His opinion of the world at all times must be, that it is a poor, empty, worthless bubble, which will soon vanish away; and even at those seasons when he feels himself too much entangled and drawn aside by worldly objects, still his judgment is not changed, and he wonders he should be so much the dupe of a bewitching strumpet. It is not so with the Formalist. Amidst his highest parade of religious pomp, so far is he from suspecting the world to be his adversary, that it is his idol. Give him plenty of the world, and in return he will give God plenty of prayers and sacraments and *some* almsdeeds, but amidst them all, the world is uppermost in his affections; though "God forbid (says he) that I should neglect my duty."

No. CXXXVII.

IT was an observation of that great ornament of the law, *Sir Mathew Hale*, that in proportion as he had sanctified the Sabbath Day, God had prospered him all the rest of the week. I fear there are few lawyers now-a-days of this good man's opinion; I should rather say, I fear there are but few who have tried his experiment; as Sunday is the great day for drawing and examining briefs, holding consultations, &c. and above all, for the pleasing amusement of receiving *retainers*. But not to look at *the law* alone; Sunday, among all ranks (persons in high life setting the pernicious example) is the principal day for feastings, visitings, travelling, &c. and of late for concerts. In a word, the Lord's day is set apart for every thing but for the Lord; and, in too many families, almost all kind of business is transacted on that day, except the great business of piety and religion. Surely, God hath a controversy with us, and will be avenged of such a nation as this, for our horrid abuse of his sacred day of rest.

It is to be hoped, however, that his Majesty's late proclamation has done some good in stemming

ming the torrent of Sabbath impiety. May magistrates be active! May ministers be earnest! May every private Christian, by precept and example, lend an hand to help forward this salutary work! and may we be as much distinguished for our national repentance and amendment, as we have been and still are for our national wickedness and profaneness! Else, without pretending to prophetic gifts, I fear I may truly say, that an heavy cloud of wrath hangs over, us, and is even now ready to burst upon this devoted land, devoted, not to God, but to sin, and on that account *to destruction*. As a nation, both Churchmen and Dissenters have departed from the pure evangelical doctrines of the reformation; and our dreadful defection in principle has produced an equally dreadful defection in practice.

Arianism, Socinianism, Pelagianism, and Arminianism are not ashamed to unveil their faces, and to woo their lovers at noon day, and many, very many unwary and unstable souls have they beguiled and espoused, to themselves; but whether we view this grand quadruple alliance of *isms*, separate or united, they have altogether produced but one frightful distorted brat, viz. practical Antinomianism. From Parents and offspring *good Lord deliver us* and our Land.—Amen and Amen.

THE

THE FOLLOWING

MEDITATIONS

WERE TRANSCRIBED

From a DIARY BOOK, which was
written about the Year 1758.

Joseph and his Brethren.

WAS the innocent Jofeph hated and defpifed of his brethren, who moved by envy, (Acts, vii. 9.) confpired his death? So was the immaculate Lamb of God hated, defpifed, and confpired againſt by his brethren the Jews, who for envy delivered him to Pilate. (Mat. xiv. 10.) Was Jofeph fold, ſtript of his raiment, and caſt into a pit? So was Chriſt both fold and ſtript; whofe death and lying in the grave is ſtrikingly typified by Jofeph's lying in the pit; the pit and the grave being uſed in ſcripture as fynonimous terms. Was Jofeph drawn out of the pit, and made ruler over a nation

that

that till then had not known him? So God would not *leave the soul of his holy one in hell*; neither *suffer him to see corruption*; but he rose again, *to be a light to lighten the Gentiles*, and was *found of them that sought him not.* Was Christ tempted, and did he overcome the temptation? So it was with Joseph, who resisted and overcame the temptations of his mistress. Did Christ suffer with two malefactors; and was the one pardoned and the other condemned? So was Joseph numbered with the transgressors, when he was imprisoned with the butler and baker of Pharoah, one of whom was pardoned, and the other condemned. Was it said of Joseph, that he shall teach his senators wisdom? How much more is this true of Christ, the Eternal Word, the Wisdom of God! Did all that was put into Joseph's hand, prosper? So it is said of Christ, that the pleasure of the Lord should prosper in his hand. Did a grievous famine prevail in other lands whilst there was plenty in Egypt, where Joseph was? So wherever Christ is not, there must of necessity be a spiritual famine; but wherever the true Joseph is, there will be bread *enough, and to spare.* Did multitudes who were ready to perish for want, flock from all parts to buy corn of Joseph? So unto Christ is *the gathering of the nations*, who breaketh the bread of life to the hungry,

hungry, and filleth the empty foul with goodnefs.

Thus much of this interefting prophetic hiftory is already accomplifhed; the remaining part of it will not perhaps be fulfilled in its fpiritual fenfe, before the time of the reftoration of the Jews; till the arrival of which happy period the yearning of Jofeph's bowels towards his barbarous brethren, who fuppofed him to be dead, and knew not that it was he that had preferved, fed, and fupported them, doth finely and ftrikingly reprefent the wonderful affection of Chrift towards his crucifiers the Jews, who though now he is eftranged from them, and they *efteem him fmitten, ftricken, and afflicted*, Ifa. 53. yet doth he ftill preferve them, and will *never leave them, nor forfake them*, but at his *fecond coming* to eftablifh his glorious kingdom in the Millenium will make himfelf known to them, with more than that amazing tendernefs wherewith Jofeph, *at the fecond time* (Acts vii. 13.) difcovered himfelf to his brethren. (Gen. xlv. 1, 2, 3, 4, 5, 6, &c.) Then fhall they look upon him whom they have pierced. Then fhall they acknowledge him to be indeed the fon of God, their much injured Meffiah, as Jofeph's brethren did look upon, and acknowledge him to be their much injured brother, the dearly beloved fon of their father in whom he was well pleafed.

At this glorious juncture (which by all the signs of the times is not far off,) the church of Jews and Gentiles, of the calling of whom Joseph's younger brother Benjamin was an eminent type, will be united, and we shall be *one fold under one shepherd Jesus Christ.*

This very remarkable history of Joseph and his brethren seems placed at the beginning of the Bible as a short summary preface containing all that should befal the Jewish nation from its rise to the end of the world.

There is yet a more particular application of this history, (especially of the latter part of it,) when Christ manifests himself to a soul that has been long in desertion, at which time there is a meeting between them, very like that of Joseph and his brethren; but as Joseph seemed for a time to use his brethren unkindly, when they came to him for corn, though ready to perish for want, yet his bowels all the while yearned most affectionately towards them; so many poor, fainting souls, that come hungering and thirsting after righteousness, seem to meet with what they are apt to think very hard treatment, as we see in the case of the psalmist, when he cries out in such bitterness of soul *hath God forgotten to be gracious? is his mercy clean gone for ever, and will he be no more intreated?* (Pf. 77.) So again, *O my God I cry*

in

in the day time, but thou hearest not, and in the night feafon alfo I take no reft. This is further exemplified in the blind man, who fat by the way fide begging. (Lu. xviii. 35, &c.) As alfo in the poor woman of Canaan. (Mat. xv. 22, &c.) Jefus at firft feems to take no notice of either of them; nay, he gives nothing but difcouraging anfwers to the latter, though he plainly fhewed them afterwards that his heart was full of love towards them all the while he feemed deaf to their intreaties. And as Jofeph's brethren were troubled at his prefence, partly through joy, and partly through a fenfe of their own ingratitude, when he faid unto them, " *I am Jofeph:*" fo when Chrift fays to a poor foul, " *I am thy falvation,*" then is that foul as it were overwhelmed, partly at the thoughts of its own unworthinefs, and partly at the torrent of facred joy that overpowers it.

THE WORLD's ESTIMATE OF CONVERSION.

SO long as a man continues carelefs about the ftate of his foul, he may pafs on fmoothly, and will meet with little or no oppofition in the broad way that leads to deftruction, if he deck himfelf with a few external duties, and live not in any

grofs

gross notorious sins, he will be looked upon as a person of great value and merit; and his piety will be highly extolled: but if he indeed take his salvation seriously to heart, and, instead of the husks of religion, be willing to feed upon the kernel, then will the devil's agents soon rise up against him, and no name will be too bad for him. Once indeed he was an honest, good sort of a man; but now he is a poor, melancholy mope, or crack-brained enthusiast. Once he did every thing as he ought; but now he carries matters a great deal too far. Now do his anxious relations, and others that go by the name of his friends, begin to admonish him of his error; and exhort him not to make himself particular, telling him to beware of being righteous overmuch; and that there is no need of all that extraordinary precifeness that he is apt to imagine; that he is low-spirited and ought to take his innocent diversions freely, and go into company, and be like other people. Nay, some poor souls, under strong convictions of sin, have been treated as if they laboured under some bodily disease; the physician hath been sent for, and in vain exerted all his skill, till Christ, the great physician of souls, has poured his sweet balm of Gilead into the sore; and, like the good Samaritan, by the wine of his blood, and the oil of his spirit, hath healed all those

those cankering wounds, which he met with among the thieves of this world.

So also it frequently happens, that when carnal, decent, dead-hearted Formalists are afraid of their relations becoming real vital Christians, that they get daubing, unawakened clergymen to talk to them of the danger and absurdity of running into extremes, and point out to them particular persons as laudable examples for their imitation, telling them to observe Mr. Such-an-one, who, though a very charitable, good man, and universally esteemed by all that know him, does nevertheless take his innocent pleasures freely, and thinks a prudent compliance with the world highly necessary. But it must be replied, that the universal esteem any man may meet with, is by no means a scripture mark of his being a disciple of Jesus Christ, who pronounces woe against all the world's favorites; (Lu. vi. 26.) and tells us expressly, that the world will always love its own, and speak well of them, and hate those whom he hath chosen out of the world. (John, xv. 19.) But on the contrary, it is those that are persecuted by the world, and are reviled and reproached of men, whom our dear Redeemer declares to be the heirs of Heaven. Blessed are they, saith he, which are persecuted for righteousness sake, for theirs is the kingdom of Heaven. Blessed are ye
when

when men shall revile you and persecute you, and shall say all manner of evil against you falsely for my sake. Rejoice and be exceeding glad, for great is your reward in Heaven. Mat. v. 10, 11. So also St. Paul assures us, that the friendship of the world is enmity with God; and whosoever will be a friend of the world, is the enemy of God.

Now, let any one judge from these express texts of scripture, whether to be well or ill spoken of by the world, is the truest mark of a Christian.

But although the word of truth assures us that in the world we shall have tribulation, (John xvi. 33.) and that all who will live godly in Christ Jesus shall suffer persecution; (2 Tim. iii. 12) yet our Savior tells us not to marvel if the world hate us; (1 John iii. 13.) hereby plainly intimating that this hatred of his true disciples might well afford them matter of astonishment: for what more unlikely than that so long as a person continues a rebel to God, a slave to his lusts and appetites, a bitter enemy to mankind in general, and particularly to all his acquaintance, by doing what is in his power to keep them from their only good, and to encourage them to go on in the broad way that leads to destruction, what more unlikely than that a person of this stamp should

should be universally loved and esteemed? Again what more unlikely than that such an one should no sooner be made sensible of his error, acknowledge his ingratitude to his Maker and Redeemer, become meek, humble, affable, and loving to all; experience the happiness of his change, pity the misery of those who are still under the delusion, be desirous of rescuing them from the jaws of hell, and of making them partakers of that real heartfelt joy, which is the companion of the established Christian; what more unlikely, I say, than that a man should no sooner undergo such a change, than he should be most cordially hated by the generality of people; and that they should fall upon him like ravenous wolves? Yet, however extraordinary this may seem, daily experience shews it to be true.

But though the Christian cannot help sincerely pitying his persecutors, and praying to God to turn their hearts, yet in some senses he may look upon them as his real friends; 1*st*. Because they afford him a distinguishing mark of his being in the right way to glory, which without the assistance of their malice he could not have obtained. 2*dly*. Because it is oftentimes with a Child of God, as with a sluggish horse, he must be spurred on when he is inclinable to stand still; so the reproaches and outcries of the world, are excellent

lent incitements to encourage and stimulate the followers of Christ, to press forward in the ways of holiness; and in proportion as they are persecuted by the world, to seek closer fellowship and communion with him who hath overcome the world for their sakes, and is able to keep them from the evil of it.

A MEDITATION, ON WISD. ch. v.

" This was he whom we had sometimes in de-
" rision, and as a proverb of reproach.
" We fools accounted his life madness; and his
" end to be without honor."
Wisdom of Solomon, ch. v.

THESE words are, by the author of the Book of Wisdom, put into the mouths of those, who, in the days of their health and gaiety, took pleasure in reproaching and ridiculing the people of God, as a company of poor, despicable, moping fools, or downright madmen, to forsake all the mirth and jollity that this life might have afforded them, in order to trust to the uncertainty of what might happen hereafter.

The scene represents the day of judgment; the actors are the above-mentioned scoffers, who in this doleful tragedy, begin to have very different notions of things, than what they had when playing their parts in that farce wherein they shone so brightly upon the stage of this world. For then they could find no better language for the godly, than *ye fools*, and *ye madmen*; but now the case is quite altered. The righteous is proved to be the only wise man; and they are constrained to call themselves, *we fools*, and *we madmen*.

But let us not suppose, that these despisers and abusers of the people of God were confined to Solomon's time: since even *God manifest in the flesh*, was reproached as a madman, and as being possessed with a devil; and the chosen vessel, St. Paul, was rudely told by a noble governor, that *he was beside himself*, when speaking that wisdom which is not of this world. Now then, if our blessed Lord himself, and the great apostle of the Gentiles were thus ill-treated and ridiculed, how much more shall the inferior servants of the household of faith be contemned, and counted the offscouring of all things?

Indeed he shews himself to be a novice in the school of Christ, or rather, I should fear, he had never received *the grace of God in truth*, who supposes that it is possible to be *a Christian alto-*
" *gether,*

gether, and not meet with rebuffs and perfecutions from a carnal world. Slander and detraction no man is proof againſt; and oftentimes the faireſt characters ſhall be the moſt foully bedaubed by the tongue of malevolence. For, as the excellent Mr. Jenks well obſerves, that "whatever any
" may talk or think of ſome being ſo good, they can
" have no enemies, but all muſt needs love them,
" it is indeed mere talk and miſtake; for if they be
" good indeed, with the holy good, the beſt and
" chief of goods (and without which none is really
" good), all that goodneſs ſhall not defend them;
" but many articles ſhall be found againſt them."

In ſhort, it is not only certain, that *all who will live godly in Chriſt Jeſus, muſt ſuffer perſecution*; (2 Tim. iii. 12.) but that ſo ſoon as a perſon comes to the right uſe of his ſenſes, the world will be ready to think him mad. This may ſeem to be an hard ſaying to many; but I am convinced, that there are few real Chriſtians but have experienced it to be true.

NATURE

NATURE STARK BLIND IN SPIRITUALS.

IT was admirably well faid "that there is more need of grace than of learning to make a Chriftian." And if we will believe the fcriptures, we may know that many things are hid from the wife and prudent, and revealed unto babes: (i. e.) Though the things of God cannot be fathomed by the wifdom of this world, yet he is pleafed to reveal them by his fpirit to fuch as are but babes in Chrift, and receive the gofpel with fimplicity and godly fincerity. Hence it frequently happens that poor, illiterate peafants, who have received the grace of God in truth, are much better judges of fpiritual matters, and much better qualified to difcourfe of them, than many learned Rabbi's, and fubtle reafoners, who have perhaps turned over one commentator after another, without attaining one grain of that knowledge whereby alone we can be wife unto falvation: for *God hath chofen the foolifh things of the world, to confound the wife* (1 Cor. 1. 27) and *the natural man receiveth not the things of the fpirit of God, for they are foolifhnefs unto him; neither can he know them becaufe*

they

they are spiritually discerned; but he that is spiritual judgeth all things. (1 Cor. 2, 14, 15.) Therefore be a man never so well skilled in languages, be he never so profound a philosopher, yet if he is still in his natural state, he is much more incapable of discovering the mysteries of that kingdom, which is *righteousness, peace, and joy in the Holy Ghost,* (Rom. 14. 17.) than a clown is of discerning the secrets of all the kingdoms of Europe. Nay farther, a man who is born blind and deaf may have a better conception of colours or sounds, than any mind unenlightened by the spirit of God can form of soul-saving things. Not but what human learning will greatly assist those that are possessed of it in the historical and prophetical parts of scripture; as well as in the knowledge of the original languages in which the sacred volume was written, yet when they come to explain *the deep things of God,* what blundering work do they make of it! perhaps giving you this, and that doctor's opinion, till they have gone through all but the right, which if they happen to meet with in any Christian author, they think too absurd to be inserted, unless it be to expose and ridicule it: therefore though grace without learning will make a Christian; yet learning without grace will only lead into errors; but when learning and grace go together, it is a blessed
thing

thing for the poffeffor, as well as for the church of God.

Was a grave, formal, unawakened profeffor, to hear the people of God talk about their experiences, their fpiritual defertions and comforts, the workings of the Holy Ghoft upon their hearts, their convictions, and humiliations, their legal terrors, and ftruggles with the fpirit of bondage, and their fweet fenfe and feeling of the fpirit of adoption, what wonderful jargon, and enthufiaftical gibberifh muft it appear to him! would he not think them *a people of a ftrange language?* and more proper objects for bedlam, than for heaven.

This confideration fhould teach real Chriftians to be cautious how they difcourfe of fuch things before the unconverted, and how they *caft their pearls before fwine.* that will either trample them under foot, or turn again and devour thofe who offer them.

SPIRITUAL DESERTIONS AND COMFORTS.

WERE we always to be exulting under the fenfible comforts of the fpirit, how little fhould we know of our own *defperately wicked hearts!*

how

how liable should we be to be puff'd up with spi‑
ritual pride, and to fancy ourselves the chief
favourites of Heaven! so that in the school of
darkness and desertion, the Christian learns many
excellent and useful lessons. Then it is, that he
ransacks his heart with diligence, and finds it to
be a foul sink of iniquity, a *Babylon of unclean
birds and spirits.* Then it is, that he sees his ut‑
ter inability *to do any thing of himself to help him‑
self,* and that his *sufficiency is of God.* Then
doth he plainly perceive the folly of putting any
confidence in the arm of flesh, and that he must
trust in the Lord, and stay himself upon his God.
Then doth he learn *to speak a word in season to
him that is weary,* and to tell others from his
own experience that *man doth not live by bread
alone,* but *by every word that proceedeth out of the
mouth of God.* Again; it is in the state of deser‑
tion that the Christian learns to receive spiritual
blessings with greater thankfulness, from a tho‑
rough conviction that he can as soon move a
mountain, or create a world, as kindle the least
spark of divine love in his hard, dull, dead, cold,
heart; till Christ *the sun of Righteousness arise*
upon it *with healing under his wings;* or as the
sweet canticle expresses it, he sees that *if a man
would give all the substance of his house for love, it
should utterly be contemn'd.*

Lastly,

Lastly, the faithful soul that hath experienced a long, and painful absence from her beloved, and has been seeking him beside *the shepherds tents*, (the ordinances,) and enquiring for him amongst *the watchmen*, (the ministers) though without success; as soon as she hears his *sweet* and *well known voice*, and perceives him to be *looking forth at the windows*, and *shewing himself through the lattice*; then will she *arise* and *open* the *door* of her *heart* to her *beloved bridegroom*, for fear he should *withdraw himself*, and will not suffer *his head to be filled with dew, and his locks with the drops of the night.* Then will she *hold him fast*, and *will not let him go*, till she has brought him into her *mother's house* (the church), where *his banner over her will be love*; and the language of the spouse's soul, " *I am my beloved's, and my beloved is mine.*

[*See this extracted from different parts of the canticle.*]

AN

HYMN,

CONTAINING THE

AUTHOR'S OWN EXPERIENCE:

COMPOSED ONE NIGHT WHEN HE COULD NOT SLEEP.

God my Maker giveth Songs in the Night. Job, xxxv. 10.

I.

MY guilty foul, how long befet,
  With terrors all around;
Whilft law and juftice claim'd their debt,
  But I no payment found.

II.

In works and duties long I try'd
  Some inward peace to find;
The more I ftrove, the more I cry'd,
  Ah! much is left behind.

III.

My weary foul the tafk renew'd,
   And fain the prize would win;
But when my righteous deeds I view'd,
   I found each deed was fin.

IV.

Now Sinai's thunders louder roll,
   And fenfe proclaim'd me loft;
Diftracting anguifh feiz'd my foul,
   And Hope gave up the ghoft!

V.

At length I heard the gofpel found,
   O joyful found to me!
Jehovah juft may ftill be found,
   And fet th' ungodly free.

VI.

That precious blood, which faith applies,
   In fpight of hell and fin,
My guilty confcience pacifies,
   And fpreads fweet peace within.

VII.

My spotless Savior liv'd for me,
  On him my sins were laid;
And whilst I view him rise, I see
  Each mite was fully paid.

VIII.

Ascended now to God on high,
  Above th' aetherial skies,
He bids me boldly to draw nigh,
  And all my wants supplies.

IX.

Though base back-slidings me reprove,
  He those backslidings heals:
Displays his never-changing love,
  And all his grace reveals.

X.

Say, dearest shepherd, tell me why,
  To me this wond'rous love;
That such a poor lost sheep as I,
  Such matchless grace should prove?

XI.

Reasons I seek, but seek in vain,
For none I e'er shall know:
Then seek no more, since this is plain,
That God wou'd have it so.

FINIS.

BOOKS *printed for, and fold by* J. MATHEWS, No. 18, *Strand.*

1. SURGICAL TRACTS, containing a Treatife upon Ulcers of the Legs; in which former Methods of Treatment are candidly examined, and compared with one more rational and fafe; -effected without Reft and Confinement; together with Hints on a fuccefsful Method of treating fome Scrophulous Tumours, and the Mammary-Abfcefs, and Sore Nipples of Lying-in Women. The 2d Edition enlarged; to which are now added, Obfervations on the more common Diforders of the Eye, and on Gangrene, by Michael Underwood, M. D. Price in boards, 4s. 3d.

2. A TREATISE on the DISEASES of CHILDREN, with Directions for the Management of Infants from the Birth; efpecially fuch as are brought up by Hand, by Michael Underwood, M. D. Price fewed, 3s.

3. PRINCIPLES of SURGERY, Part the Firft, by JOHN PEARSON, Surgeon to the Lock Hofpital, and to the Public Difpenfary. Price in boards, 5s.

DIVINITY.

4. A Key to open Scripture Metaphors, in four Books, by Mr. Benjamin Keach; recommended by feveral eminent Divines of the prefent Day. Price 1l. 11s. 6d.

5. HORÆ SOLITARIÆ, or Effays upon the effential Divinity, and proper Perfonality of the SON and HOLY SPIRIT, confidered in connection with their refpective Offices in human Redemption, and with the Faith and Practice of the Chriftian Life; to which are added brief Accounts of the Herefies which have arifen upon the Divinity of thefe PERSONS; and alfo an Hiftorical ESSAY upon the DOCTRINE OF THE TRINITY, both as it ap-

P 3   peared

BOOKS printed for J. MATHEWS.

peared before the Chriſtian Æra, and as it hath been promulgated and corrupted in various Parts of the World, in 2 vols. 8vo. the 2d Edit. with large Additions. Price in boards, 12s. or 14s. bound.—*N. B.* The above Work is earneſtly recommended by the Rev. Mr. Romaine.

6. Fifty-two Sermons on the Baptiſmal Covenant, the Creed, the Ten Commandments, and other important Subjects of Practical Religion, in 2 vol. 8vo. by Samuel Walker, of Truro, A. B. Price in boards 10s. or 12s. bound.

7. The Chriſtian, being a Courſe of practical Sermons, by Samuel Walker, of Truro, A. B. Price 2s. 6d.

8. A Compendious View of natural and revealed Religion, in 7 Books, interſperſed with ſerious Addreſſes to the Conſciences of the Readers, in 1 vol. large 8vo. by John Brown. Price in boards, 5s.

9. A brief Concordance to the Holy Scriptures of the Old and New Teſtament, by John Brown. Price bound 2s 6d.

10. A brief View of the Figures and Explication of the Metaphors contained in the Scriptures, by John Brown. Price bound, 3s.

11. The Chriſtian Journal, by John Brown. Price bound, 3s.

12. The Chriſtian, the Student, and Paſtor, exemplified in the Lives of ſeveral eminent Divines, by John Brown. Price bound 2s. 6d.

13. The dying Experience of the Rev. Mr. John Brown, late of Haddington, with his dying Addreſſes to his Wife and Children, and Advice to his Congregation, will be ſpeedily publiſhed.

14. Beart's Vindication of the Eternal Law and Everlaſting Goſpel. The 3d Edit. with a Preface and Notes, by C. Decoetlogon. Price ſewed, 2s. 6d. or bound, 3s.

15. Prayers

BOOKS printed for J. MATHEWS.

15. Prayers and Offices of Devotion for Families and for particular Perſons upon moſt Occaſions, by Benjamin Jenks, the 21ſt Edit. Price bound 3s.

16. A Companion for the Chriſtian, in his Field and Garden. Price bound, 2s. ſewed 1s. 6d.

17. The Chriſtian Remembrancer, or ſhort Reflections upon the Faith, Life and Conduct of a real Chriſtian; the 2d Edit. on a larger Type. Price 2s. ſewed; bound 2s. 6d. The above two by the Author of Horæ Solitariæ.

18. The Pilgrim's Progreſs from this World to that which is to come, by John Bunyan, complete in 2 Parts, a new Edition, divided into Chapters, to which are added explanatory Notes. Together with the Life of the Author, containing many new and curious Particulars, by G. Burder, Miniſter of the Goſpel at Coventry, adorned with ten neat Copper Plates. Price bound, 3s. 6d.

19. Deep Things of God; or Milk and Strong Meat: containing ſpiritual and experimental Remarks and Meditations, ſuited to the Caſes of Babes, Young Men, and Fathers in Chriſt: particularly to ſuch as are under Trials and Temptations, and who feel the Plague of their own Hearts. Price in boards, 2s. bound, 2s 6d.

20. A new Edit. of the Juſtice of God in the Damnation of Sinners, explained, illuſtrated, and proved in a Sermon, upon Rom. iii. 19. by Jonathan Edwards, A. M. late Preſident of New Jerſey College, New England, reviſed and corrected by C. De Coetlogon, A. M. Price 6d. will be ſpeedily publiſhed.

21. A Preſent for Your Neighbour, or the Right Knowledge of GOD, and of OURSELVES opened, in a plain, practical, and experimental manner, by Sir Richard Hill, Bart. The eighth Edition. Price 3d. or one Guinea per Hundred.

22. A

BOOKS printed for J. MATHEWS.

22. A Short Catechism, containing the Fundamental Principles of Christianity, originally published in the German Tongue, for the use of the Schools and Churches in the Palatinate; afterwards translated into French, for the Benefit of the Protestant Cantons in Switzerland: and now translated into English, with a Preface, by Sir Richard Hill, Bart. Price 6d. stitched, and 9d. bound. or 2l. 2s. per Hundred stitched.

23. Truth defended, or a Vindication of the eternal Law, and everlasting Gospel. Wherein the Immutability of the Law; its high Demands; the Incapacity of Man for obeying it, in his fallen State, are asserted and proved. The Suretyship of Christ; his Obeying and Suffering; are maintained and defended. And the Concernment of Faith in Justification, is opened and explained. In the second Part, Justification before Faith is stated and limited; and Justification by Faith asserted and proved. The Offer of Christ to Sinners; the Usefulness of Exhortations, and Motives in preaching the Gospel is vindicated: and some other weighty Points are briefly discussed. By John Beart. The third Edition; illustrated with explanatory Notes, and Quotations at large: with an Apology to the Reader, by the Rev. Mr. Charles De Coetlogon, A. M. Price sewed, 2s. 6d. or bound 3s.

24. A Sketch of the distinguishing Graces of the Christian Character, as originating from the Holy Spirit's secret, yet efficacious Influence upon the Minds of Men: with a rational Inquiry into the Reality and Nature of Divine Influences. By Philip Gurdon, M. A. Fellow of Magdalen College, Oxford. Price 2s 6d. sewed.

25. A new Edition enlarged, of a Lash at Enthusiasm: in a Dialogue between two Ladies, chiefly relative to a certain popular Preacher, founded on
real

BOOKS printed for J. MATHEWS.

real Facts. To which is now first added, a Dialogue between four very good old Ladies over a comfortable Game at Quadrille. Price 6d.

26. A short and candid Addrefs to the Religious Society called Baptifts in general, and to thofe of that Denomination at Reading, Berks, in particular. Price 6d.

27. Chriftian Memoirs, or a Review of the prefent State of Religion in England, in the Form of a new Pilgrimage to the Heavenly Jerufalem: containing, by Way of allegorical Narrative, a great Variety of Dialogues on the moft interefting Subjects, and Adventures of eminently religious Perfons, by W. Shrubfole. Price fewed 3s. 6d.

28. Self difclaimed, and Chrift exalted; a fermon preached at Philadelphia, before the Synod of New York, by David Boftwick, A. M. Price 6d.

29. A fair and rational Vindication of the Rights of Infants to the Ordinance of Baptifm, by David Boftwick, A. M. A new Edition. Price 4d.

30. A Treatife on the Extent of the Death of Chrift, being an Abridgment of Dr. Owen's Death of Death in the Death of Chrift, with a recommendatory Preface by the Rev. Mr. Charles De Coetlogon, A. M. Price 1s.

31. Some Account of the State of Religion in London, in four Letters to a Friend in the Country, in which are drawn many ftriking Characters of real and nominal Chriftians, fhewing the happy Iffue of the former, and the awfull Declenfions and Falls of the latter. Defigned to fhew the Profeffors of the Gofpel the Greatnefs of their Privileges, and to excite them to a correfpondent Conduct, as the only means of fecuring the Continuance of them.

32. Murrey's Clofet Devotions, bound, 2s. 6d.

33. A Treatife on Affurance, by the late Rev. Thomas Brooks. A new Edition. Price 1s. 6d.
fewed,

BOOKS printed for J. MATHEWS.

fewed, 2s. bound; and on fine Paper, 2s. fewed, 2s. 6d. bound.

34. Bofton's Crook in the Lot, bound, 1s.

35. Jefus Triumphant in the Converfion and Death of Anna Catharine Merks, executed at Rotterdam in Holland, with a brief Account of her Life. Price 9d.

36. A Choice Drop of Honey from the Rock of Chrift. Price 3d. or 1l. 1s. per Hundred.

37. A Warning to Englifh Proteftants, on Occafion of the prefent more than ordinary Growth of Popery: containing many valuable Particulars, and adorned with a Frontifpiece, reprefenting the burning of Catharine Cawches and her two Daughters. Price 6d.

38. The Way to be Happy in a Miferable World. Price 2d. or 14s. per Hundred.

39. The Chriftian Dignity, or the humbleft Believer the greateft Man. Price 3d. or 1l. 1s. per Hundred.

40. A Chriftmas Box for the Heart. Price 2d. or 14s. per Hundred.

41. A Serious Addrefs to the truly religious of all Denominations, upon the Temper and Conduct of Profeffors, in Times of Public Difturbance. Price 3d. or 1l. 1s. per Hundred.

42. The Converfion and religious Experience of the Rev. Jonathan Edwards, of New England. Price 2d. or 14s. per Hundred.

43. CHRIST IS ALL. With a Preface by Dr. Peckwell. Neatly fewed in marble Paper, 4d. or 1l. 7s. per Hundred; and 6d. bound in Sheep, or 2l. 2s. per Hundred.

44. A Memoir of fome principal Circumftances in the Life and Death of the Reverend and learned Auguftus Toplady, B. A. late Vicar of Broad Hembury, Devon: to which is added, written by himfelf,

BOOKS printed for J. MATHEWS.

himself, The Dying Believer's Addrefs to his Soul, and his own laft Will and Teftament. The 3d Edition. Price 6d.

44. An Elegiac Poem in Blank Verfe, on the Death of the Rev. Mr. A. M. Toplady, A. B. By John Fellows, Author of the Hiftory of the Bible in Verfe, &c. Price 6d.

45. An Elegy on the Death of the Rev. Mr. A. M. Toplady, A. B. By T. W. Price 6d.

The following eighteen Pieces, writtten by the Rev. Auguftus Toplady, B. A.

1. THE fecond Edition, enlarged, of the Church of England, vindicated from the Charge of Arminianifm. Price 1s. 6d.

2. The fecond Edition, improved, of the Doctrine of abfolute Predeftination, ftated and afferted. Price 2s.

3. A Letter to Mr. John Wefley. Price 6d.

4. A fecond Edition of a Caveat againft unfound Doctrines, a Sermon. Price 9d.

5. The fecond Edition of Jefus feen of Angels; and God's Mindfulnefs of Man : Three Sermons, preached at Broad Hembury, Devon, Dec. 25, 1770. Price 1s. 6d.

6. Free Thoughts on the Application to Parliament for the Abolition of Ecclefiaftical Subfcriptions. Price 6d.

7. More Work for John Wefley. Price 1s. 6d.

8. Clerical Subfcription no Grievance, a Sermon. Price 6d.

9. Hiftoric Proof, 2 Vols. 8vo. in Boards, Price 10s.

10. Free-will and Merit fairly examined, or Men not their own Saviours. Price 6d.

11. Good News from Heaven, or, The Gofpel a joyful Sound. Price 6d. 12. The

BOOKS printed for J. MATHEWS.

12. The Scheme of Christian and Philosophical Necessity. Price in Boards, 3s.

13. Joy in Heaven, and the Creed of Devils, two Sermons, 1s.

14. Moral and Political Moderation, a Fast Sermon. Price 6d.

15. Collection of Hymns for Public and Private Worship, 1776. Price bound 3s.

16. A Fifth Edition of his Dying Avowal. Price 1d.

17. His Posthumous Works, containing, 1st. Excellent Passages selected from the Writings of Eminent Divines, &c. 2. Short Memorials of God's gracious Dealings with his Soul. 3. Collections of Letters. 4. A Short History of England. Price in boards 5s.

18. The Gleanings of the Vintage, being several Essays and Meditations selected from the Manuscripts of Periodical Papers, written by Augustus Montague Toplady, with a Preface by Dr. Peckwell. Price 1s.

⁎ Where may be had, Books in all the Sciences and Branches of Polite Literature, and particularly those of evangelical and experimental Divinity, both new, and second-hand.

†‡† Bibles, and Common Prayers of all Kinds and Sizes: Likewise a great Variety of Hymn Books, by Mess. Whitefield, Madan, Peckwell, Newton, Dr. Watts, &c. in different neat and elegant Bindings; with Stationary Wares of all Sorts; Ledgers and Accompt Books, &c. &c.

☞ Books neatly Bound—Money for Libraries or Parcels of Books.

N. B. Country Booksellers, Schoolmasters and Shopkeepers, served with Books and Stationaries, Wholesale, on the lowest Terms, and with Punctuality.

www.ingramcontent.com/pod-product-compliance
Lightning Source LLC
Chambersburg PA
CBHW020846160426
43192CB00007B/800